PRAISE FOR MARK NEPO

"Mark Nepo is one of the finest spiritual guides of our time."

PARKER J. PALMER
author of *A Hidden Wholeness* and *The Courage to Teach*

"Mark Nepo is a Great Soul. His resonant heart—and his frank and astonishing voice—befriend us mightily on this mysterious trail."

NAOMI SHIHAB NYE
author of *You and Yours, 19 Varieties of Gazelle:
Poems of the Middle East*, and *Red Suitcase*

"Mark Nepo is an eloquent spiritual teacher."

HERBERT MASON
professor emeritus of history and religious thought
at Boston University and translator of *Gilgamesh*

"Mark Nepo is one of our national treasures. That is because Mark inhabits that rare and beautiful consciousness that enables him to express the language of the soul. The words and energy flowing from the font of his heart not only make our lives more beautiful, but heal us."

REV. ED BACON
author, *8 Habits of Love*

"Mark Nepo is someone who walks through this confusing and sometimes dark world holding up a lantern and lighting the way. His voice helps us find pathways where we might have believed that no pathway could possibly exist. He is more than simply brave and more than simply wise; he is deeply kind— because he understands that kindness is the most courageous act of wisdom there is. I can say with all certainty that I would follow this man anywhere his words want to take us."

ELIZABETH GILBERT
author of *Eat, Pray, Love* and *Big Magic*

"Mark Nepo joins a long tradition of truth-seeking, wild-hearted poets—Rumi, Walt Whitman, Emily Dickinson, Mary Oliver—and deserves a place in the center of the circle with them."   ELIZABETH LESSER
author of *Broken Open: How Difficult Times Can Help Us Grow* and *Marrow*; cofounder of Omega Institute

"Nepo is a consummate storyteller with a rare gift for making the invisible visible."   PUBLISHERS WEEKLY

"Mark Nepo has a great heart. His poems are good company."
COLEMAN BARKS
translator of *The Essential Rumi*

"Mark Nepo has a rare quality of writing, one that fills you up even as it drops you into emptiness. Through his sensibilities we touch what is human: he plucks at our heartstrings with naked candor and metaphorical mastery."   JULIE CLAYTON
New Consciousness Review

"Mark Nepo is a rare being—a poet who does not overuse language, a wise man without arrogance, a teacher who always speaks with compassion, and an easygoing love-to-listen-to-him storyteller."   JAMES FADIMAN, PHD
cofounder, Institute for Transpersonal Psychology

"Mark Nepo's work is as gentle and reliable as the tides, and as courageous as anyone I've known in looking deeply into the mysteries of the self."   MICHAEL J. MAHONEY
author of *Human Change Processes*

PRAISE FOR
THE WAY UNDER THE WAY

"Mark Nepo's poems are like rare wine that directly nourishes the soul. These are stories of the heart, of brokenness that heals, of grief that awakens us to joy. They remind us of what is essential and sacred, of what we share in the depths of our humanity. Rather than offering answers, they open our questions to the greater mystery of what it means to be alive, to feel. His words welcome us to witness the wonder of who we really are."

LLEWELLYN VAUGHAN-LEE, PHD
Sufi teacher, author of *For Love of the Real*,
and editor of *Spiritual Ecology*

"When I read Mark Nepo's luminous, meditative poems, one word stands tall in the mind and silence that follows—BEFRIEND. He does not avert his eyes from the difficult moment or the lost hour. He stays steady to feel the magnificence again. And somehow, organically and instinctively, he is able to pass that hopeful calm on to us, in ways we desperately need, these and all days."

NAOMI SHIHAB NYE
author of *Words Under the Words*

PRAISE FOR *INSIDE THE MIRACLE*

"In *Inside the Miracle*, Mark Nepo gathers almost thirty years of writing, teaching and thinking about suffering, healing and wholeness, drawing on his own transformative experience with illness. With everyday lessons and hard-earned wisdom, he has given us a beautiful testament to the resilience of the human heart, and a guide to facing life's challenges with strength, grace and gratitude."   ARIANNA HUFFINGTON
author of *Thrive* and *The Sleep Revolution*

"*Inside the Miracle* is simply the best book I have read in years. Mark Nepo invites us to live a human life, fully, joyously, and without reservation, using all our experiences and vulnerabilities as a precious opportunity to encounter and serve the Mystery. He has blessed us all."   RACHEL NAOMI REMEN, MD
author of *Kitchen Table Wisdom*
and *My Grandfather's Blessings*

"*Inside the Miracle* will be a miracle for those who read it, especially those going through a difficult time, a big change, a loss, a confusion, a trial by fire. That means everyone born human. Our trials may differ in heat and length, but at the core, we are the same. We need each other, we need insight, and we need help. This book is help. It helps me every time I pick it up and read a poem or a teaching or the brave story of Mark Nepo's descent and rebirth."   ELIZABETH LESSER
author of *Broken Open: How Difficult Times Can Help Us Grow*
and *Marrow*; cofounder of Omega Institute

"In the canyon of his soul, scoured into truth by pain and uncertainty, joy and Mystery, Nepo navigates the deeper currents with prose and poetry that masterfully invites us to those places where only rarely language can reach. Relentlessly refusing to resolve paradox into mere piety, this book is a rare soul-confirming and soul-stretching gift."

SHARON DALOZ PARKS
author of *Big Questions, Worthy Dreams*

"With a hard-won heart, Mark Nepo takes us *Inside the Miracle* of our radiant and fragile human life. In every page, Mark reveals the universal in the personal, intimating the wholeness that is best expressed in paradox. This book is raw and painful and indestructibly hopeful. It tells us what we already know in fresh and surprising moments of recognition. This is a gift which we can open endlessly."

BRUCE TIFT
author of *Already Free*

THINGS
THAT
JOIN
THE SEA
AND
THE SKY

THINGS THAT JOIN THE SEA AND THE SKY

FIELD NOTES ON LIVING

MARK NEPO

sounds true
BOULDER, COLORADO

Sounds True
Boulder, CO 80306

Published 2017

Cover design by Jennifer Miles
Book design by Beth Skelley

Cover image © jumpingsack; shutterstock.com

Printed in Canada

Library of Congress Cataloging-in-Publication Data
Names: Nepo, Mark, author.
Title: Things that join the sea and the sky : field notes on living / Mark Nepo.
Description: Boulder, CO : Sounds True, 2017. | Includes bibliographical references.
Identifiers: LCCN 2017011750 (print) | LCCN 2017031679 (ebook) |
    ISBN 9781622039005 (ebook) | ISBN 9781622038992 (pbk.)
Subjects: LCSH: Life—Miscellanea.
Classification: LCC BD431 (ebook) | LCC BD431 .N36 2017 (print) |
    DDC 204/.32—dc23
LC record available at https://lccn.loc.gov/2017011750

10 9 8 7 6 5 4 3 2 1

for Ryōkan
who cried on the six-hundred-year-old manuscript of Dogen . . .

for Neruda and the coal miner
who came out of the earth and called him brother . . .

for Whitman
who volunteered as a Civil War medic for both sides . . .

for Rilke
who stared at the panther in the cage
and saw that the bars go both ways . . .

We could all learn from the flatfish.
They spend their days
scavenging in the mud
but their eyes
never leave Heaven.
They're ready for anything.
LAKE SAGARIS

CONTENTS

HOW WE MAKE OUR WAY

THREADING INNER AND OUTER:
THE PRACTICE OF JOURNALING

THE WHAT AND THE HOW

I n early March 2002, we went to the Union. Stefon Harris, the great vibes player, was sitting in with the Western Michigan Jazz Quartet. We arrived early to get a table up front, so we could see his hands. The place filled, and as they began, I felt this smile wash over my entire being. It's what I always feel when tucked inside a small club as music starts to swirl its sweet, unseeable smoke.

Stefon touched an inner chord right away. It might have been two notes an octave apart. They pierced any hesitation that had clung to me throughout the day. I was fresh again and thankful. The music opened us further as the sax player rode his first solo. Suddenly, I fell into one of those moments where life shows itself as always just beginning. We weren't just watching. We weren't just listening. We were part of the song of life starting all over again. It made me want to write a book about joy. I closed my eyes, and the sax player quieted his roll of notes, which the piano player picked up as if they'd handed them off. It made me laugh. It felt like the bough of a fallen tree letting go at the top of a waterfall, its branches gently going over.

Then, it struck me. Joy is the name for all the things that join the sea and the sky. In that instant, I met this book. Their jazz inspired my jazz. It's how these things work. One bird is flushed out of hiding by a sudden streak of light, and all the birds nearby are sent flapping into the open. So let's not talk about theories or concepts. I just know that joy is *the what* and the jazz of unscripted living is *the how*. What we love doesn't seem to matter. It's all a holy excuse to love the world and ourselves back together.

*

I started this book fifteen years ago, when I was fifty-one. What you just read is where it began. Like all books, it came alive and had ideas of its own. My initial impulse was to reach for joy, but you'll see that my sense of joy has deepened: I now experience joy in the oceanic trenches of feeling. Though when struggling, like the rest of us, it's hard to keep my head above water. But that's the point. We're asked to go below: to swim and drift in the deep where my breath and your breath and the breath of the Universe are one. This depth has taught me that joy is not the stillness waiting at the end of difficult feelings but the sea of Being that *holds* all feelings, from which the thousand moods we undergo surface like waves to engage us in the world. To my surprise, I discovered along the way that the life of feeling, when entered like a sea, holds us with the mystery of its buoyancy.

These pages are drawn from my ongoing journal of many years. And so, this thematic reader is one of my most intimate books, a travelogue of my conversation with the Universe, a mix of inner reflections, questions, and stories that have come to teach me how to be here.

I have gathered these reflections into themes we're all asked to face, thresholds we're all asked to cross, though no one can tell us how. At most, we can bear witness to each other's journey and keep each other company. There's one experience waiting if you should read these passages in order, the way you might follow a path to the sea. But each section stands alone as well, so you can go to each directly, depending on what you're faced with today. On the whole, these passages explore how we open and close and fall down and get up, given the storms and clearings that come our way. The conversation they evoke acknowledges life's difficulties, while trying to uncover the pathways to resilience and peace that have always been waiting under our trouble, if we can find them.

At the end of the book, I offer an essay about the nature and gift of journaling, followed by journaling guidelines, and a hundred journal questions to work with. All to encourage you to engage in your own conversation with the Universe.

This book contains raw moments of sinking and being lifted, intimate accounts of being thrown into feeling and depth. I share how I've been stretched into wondering about my life and the lives of others, in this ongoing push and pull in a Universe that holds us, then tosses us about, only to hold us again. Under every passage, I hope you feel the common song we're each born to sing in our unique and very human way.

STOPPING
THE NOISE

When there is silence, one finds the anchor
of the Universe within oneself.
LAO TZU

Often we're cast about by the noise of the world and the noise in our heads. Often we're mesmerized by the stunning cacophony that masks itself as excitement. And though there's much to be gained for being in the world, we can't make sense of it till we stop the noise, till we go below the noise, till we go below the habit of our own thoughts. But it's impossible to be still and quiet all the time. As a whale or dolphin must break surface, only to dive back down, only to break surface again, each of us must break surface into the noise of the world, only to rest our way back into the depth of stillness, where we can know ourselves and life more deeply, until we have to break surface again. No one is ever done with this crossover between noise and stillness. Not even those committed to a contemplative life. Not even those who are blind or mute. For the noise of the mind never dies. It can only be put in perspective, quieted until we can hear the more ancient voices that give us life. At every turn, we need to stop the noise, our own and everyone else's, not to retreat from the world but to live more fully in it.

QUIETING THE THIEVES

Today I am sad, or so I thought. But more I am tired of keeping up with all that doesn't matter. I'm sipping coffee, listening to rain. I like watching the leaves hang in long weather. I like to close my eyes and feel the rain quiet the earth. I welcome that quieting. I like to have my habits of going here and there interrupted. I was caught in the rain when coming here. The cool blotches sink in all over. The many lists I carry in my shirt are wet. I take them out to dry, and all the tasks have blurred. At last. Unreadable. Forgettable. We carry these lists near our heart and finger them like worry beads. It doesn't matter what is on them. They are the thieves, and it is the insidious virtue to have everything in order *before* we live that is the greatest thief. I feel the rain drip down my neck. I think I'm becoming unfinished.

BRING ME CLOSE

When I stop, the smallest things make me weep: the afternoon light dusting our dog's face, the beads of rain darkening the head of St. Francis in the neglected garden, and my father's stroke-laden tongue falling through the phone. The ache of being here reveals itself as the heartbeat of Eternity. I hear it in the throng of birds beaten back by wind, in the wall of silence that crumbles between old friends too stubborn to forgive, and in the swollen minds on the train trying to find their way home. The ache of being here undoes my need for fences.

Short Wisdom
on a Long Planet

We keep turning one thing into another and calling it progress. We keep machining the beauty off of things as they are, creating more and more things to hide in, as if that will let us live longer. We keep burrowing into everything but ourselves: churning trees into lumber, animals into meat, wind into electricity, vegetables into remedies, and silence into noise; turning the earth, continent by continent, into one giant anthill. We keep eating our way through the arms of the Universe, desperate for something large and quiet to hold us.

SPEECHLESS

I pause under that summer tree, the one that feels like a friend, as my dog wonders why we've stopped. She was trotting in such rhythm. But when this still, I wonder what part of me, way down, remains untouched by dream or memory? What drop of being remains out of reach of the opinions of others? When up close, each thing reveals its shimmer. And it's the unexpected closeness that holds everything together. The light spreads across my dog's face, her eyes so devoted to wherever I want to go. Can I be this devoted to the pull of life? Last month, I saw a dolphin and her calf slip back into the surf, and the pucker of the sea where they went under said, *This is what it feels like to shimmer and go speechless.* There's a closeness we recognize in everything simple, as if we knew everything at the moment of our birth, and living is how we remember it all, piece by broken piece. It can happen when I stop to pick up what you drop in the supermarket. As your eyes shimmer, I realize we've known each other forever, though we just met.

OUR HANDS

Sometimes, with no warning, we suffer an earthquake and have to remake the ground beneath us. Someone we love may leave or die or think us cruel when we are kind. Sometimes the tools we need break or are stolen or simply stop working, and we have to invent more. Sometimes it feels like we can't get through, that the phone won't get reception, and the computer gets jammed. And sometimes what gets through is partial and misunderstood. It's then we're forced to go barefoot and refind our hands. Sometimes we're asked to drift away from the crowd in order to be found by what we love.

OVER AND OVER

I'm not afraid of dying, but losing those I love. I can't quite imagine the world without them. Like waking to a rip in the sky through which the sun might leave. The only thing that helps is to go below the noise. There, I listen to the same piece of music day after day. I play it over and over till the squirrel in my head stops chewing and my heart admits it's tired of why. So many things show their beauty when we go quiet. So many truths are present when we look up from under our trouble. To fall below the world while still living in the world makes us remember that the truth that waits under our opinions is our home. So tell me, am I home? Are you home? When was the last time you looked up from under your trouble? And when will the fugitive we hide inside accept that our self-worth was there all along? What sort of rain will make the seed inside our head grow?

This Is How

When we can open our hearts and work with what we're given, loving what's before us, life stays possible. Then, through effort and grace, we do what we can with what we have. And when exhausted by all that's in the way, we're faced with the chance to accept and love what's left, which is everything. This is how we discover that Heaven is on Earth.

Unraveling
Our Fear

I am troubled by my shapeless fears. My God, these anxieties!
Who can live in the modern world without catching his share of them?

VINCENT VAN GOGH

I was born when all I once
feared—I could love.

THE FEMALE SUFI SAINT RABIA OF BASRA

Fear has been a great and unasked-for teacher. At every step of my cancer journey, fear was there to greet me like a dark elder, nudging me closer to all I was afraid of. I was continually forced to face what I feared with no instruction. At the bottom of every fear, when I could reach it, was my want not to die. I think all fear unravels to our want to be here. When we can get through the rush of fear, when we can endure its intensity, its real gift shows. For under all fear, no matter how legitimate or inflated, is the shimmer and glow of how precious it is to be alive. If seen all the way through, fear allows us to live as if we mean it. More often, fear hangs around like a nagging cold or toothache we can't seem to get rid of. It can discolor everything and agitate our soul. An important practice then is how to unravel our fear when it wraps itself around us, which it will.

OFFERING

We fist up to weather the days, though no one told us it has to be this way. We just constrict to keep what is tender from being hurt. If blessed, we crack and are pried open anyway, till the heart like an oyster shows its softness. Opened by time, I am more fallible, more humble, able to trip more easily into joy. Who would have guessed that the softness between us glitters like the stardust that it is. Who would have guessed that offering what is tender is what saves us.

ONCE FALLING IN

There are many things to fear, and once falling in, like tripping off the edge of a cliff, it's useless to be told not to be afraid. Yet often, like today, you and I can back away from the temptation to die before we die or feel pain before we break. I don't pretend to know how to put fear down, but these dreads on which we trip are sometimes avoidable. Some fish swim past hooks, and mice that follow light instead of cheese avoid their traps. And I know that every fear I've empowered has kept me from some wonder that would have lightened my load. I know that the damage I've done to myself by running from fear has hurt me more than the things I've feared.

On Retreat

Walking from my cabin through the frosted grass, it's very quiet. The meetinghouse is on the hill. From the field below, I see a dog on the steps. I don't have my glasses. It looks like a rottweiler or a shepherd. The old fear returns. The dog is off leash, and no one's around. I think about heading back and waiting till later. The dog looks my way. I'm not sure what to do. Its ears perk up. I keep climbing the hill, keep telling myself: that was then, this is now. I'm not the person who was so afraid. But it comes back so easily. I climb the hill like years gone by till I come in view of—where else but—*Now*. As I get closer, it's clear the beast is a small mutt. Cresting the hill, I can see it's Charlie. His old white face comes into focus, and he recognizes me as I do him. He begins to wag his tail and waddle my way. I feel foolish and stoop beside Charlie, nuzzling my face in his.

IF I COULD

Whether it's my early fear of dogs, or fear of my mother's anger, or my fear of facing cancer, or the fear of losing friendships I depend on—they all reside in a deeper fear. Regardless of what triggers it, this deeper fear is that life will swallow me with no time left to live it. When lost in this agitation, I bend the world into a mirror of dread and turn everything I touch into my fear.

At times, I'm so overwhelmed that I believe that whatever hurts me will rip a hole in my heart, and I will fall through. My experience in life has repeatedly shown that this isn't true, but that hasn't stopped the fear from hiding under all my gifts. The haunting thing is that the fear doesn't want to be abandoned any more than I do, so it's willing to transform itself, like a chameleon, into vigilance, preparedness, efficiency, or productivity.

I can see that keeping my fear pacified has not quieted it. When fearful, I'm usually moving from here to there, from past to future, from out to in, or in to out. But when in the glow of being completely where I am, I'm close to the Source of Life, and this glow of aliveness softens every circumstance, from the cup to my lip, from the window to the road. When sipping from this aliveness, my fear, like a tired wolf, goes quiet and curls up next to me. If I could, I'd hold my fear and baptize it in the lake of my heart.

THE ONLY TASK

We weren't ready for another dog, but there she was, and we said yes. Found on the streets of Kentucky with scars on her head, we named her Zuzu and drove her home. The first afternoon, her ball went under the couch. I used a yardstick to get it, and she cowered. I held her softly, saying in her ear, "No one will ever hit you again." Within days, we discovered she's afraid of other dogs. Probably had to fight for food. Now she digs in at every sudden move. We weren't ready for this. But here we are, working to teach this loving creature not to dig in, not to be afraid. Struggling to assure her that she's safe. Humbled that I, who was afraid of dogs as a boy, am asked in my sixties to teach a dog not to fear other dogs. I'm stunned at how the choreography of fate is exquisitely disguised as chance. Zuzu is asleep beside me, her eyes twitching as she dreams of her instructions: sent by the fates, like all the innocents, to find the ones who are afraid and help them teach others not to be afraid. It's the work of the world.

WE TRY, WE TRY

Everyone seeks the lightness of the future and fears the weight of the past. Everyone tumbles through the struggle of being here, playing it out on each other, because it feels too hard to face the life we're given. So often we try to flee or silence the tension of being fully here, which resisted is torment, but once accepted awakens us to a long and nameless dance. At best, we try to love our way through the struggle of being human. At worst, we try to sex or drug or own our way out of it. When that fails, we turn to violence. If blessed, the struggle enables us to build, create, and serve. This is why we're here, to be shaped by time into a tool.

DOORWAYS

A door left open is a threshold to a new world, which we often fear to go through. And a broken birdhouse can tip the baby birds into each other till the one leaned on most takes the longest to fly. I confess I've been leaned on till I forgot how to fly. But I've also been healed by simple kindnesses till others thought I was a doorway left open. They tried to go through me. In the beginning I felt violated, only because they didn't ask. Now, years later, it seems this is my purpose: to be a doorway. Yesterday I watched dawn open its chest, letting all that light pour into the world. I admit I've searched a thousand stories for their light, listening for what keeps us going. When in pain or sensing great care, I've felt a beautiful sameness, itself a doorway to the ache of being here. Today I looked into the eye of a blind horse and saw its dream of endless fields, not its fear of getting around. I know we carry dawn within us, though we search for it everywhere.

DURING THE STORM

I was dreaming of the one who doesn't see me and the one I'm afraid of, when our dog, shaken by the thunder, shimmied between us. I turned on my side and she curled into my belly. My wife in her sleep brought her legs up close. I rubbed our dog's chest slowly, and she calmed down. In about thirty minutes, the storm passed, and all that was left was the softness of holding something we love in the night. It felt like we were under the porch in Heaven, where the moon comes through the slats to remind us of our innocence. Outside, the rain was washing the world of the worries that gather between us.

BEYOND WHAT
GOES WRONG

With each passing [and passage], there is a further
wearing away of the layers or coverings that obscure
our essential selves. And so, as we say "goodbye" again
and again, we feel thinner, narrower, more naked, more
transparent, more vulnerable in a palpable, holy way.

ELESA COMMERSE

When in the middle of difficulty, it's easy to paint the whole world as difficult. When in pain, it's easy to construct a worldview of pain. When lonely, it's easy to subscribe to an alienating philosophy of existence. Then we spend hours and even years seeking to confirm the difficult existence we know. Or we rebound the other way, insisting on a much lighter, giving world, if we could only transcend the difficulties that surround us. Life has taught me that neither extreme is helpful, though I've spent many good hours lingering in each. Instead, I think we're asked to face what we're given, no matter how difficult, and to accept that life is always more than the moment we find ourselves in. In every instance, there's the truth of what we're going through and the resource of a larger, more enduring truth that's always present beyond what goes wrong. Ultimately, it's the enduring truth that helps us through.

BREAKING THE CLEARNESS

At seven-thirty this morning, my neighbor, who never talks to me, rings my bell repeatedly to let me know that my car has been broken into. It's disheartening: glass everywhere. But the morning breeze is beautiful as I crunch on slivers, peering through a shattered opening that seems a frozen scream. A rock lay on the floor near the steering wheel. Oddly, nothing was taken, not the lawn chairs in the back, or any of my CDs, just a handful of change. I can feel the randomness in this, as if it had been lightning or a tree limb falling on my car. Perhaps it was human lightning, the sudden heat of some desperate being breaking glass in the night for a handful of pennies, a broken being breaking the clearness in the dark for nothing. There are slivers in the vents, on the dash, under the seats, in the folds of maps I haven't used in years. As the day unfolds, the slivers begin to shine in a catastrophe of jewels no one can touch. My mind races with who to call and what to do. How can I possibly find all those slivers? So I go for a run, jogging around strangers on their way to work, to the post office, to the bank to pay a bill so the electric won't be shut off. I begin to sweat and breathe heavily as I dodge a sad woman smoking her cigarette and a tall man sipping his cappuccino. I jog and think, somewhere someone is making desperate love, and somewhere else someone is dreaming of making desperate love, and somewhere the sad broken being who broke my piece of clearness in the night is having breakfast or sleeping it off. And I wonder about the tensions that twist our lives. We're just a tangle of roots in the vast human garden in which things blossom and bear fruit, break and mend, seed and die. I'm tired and thrown off my rhythm. But running home, I stand before my car, before the shattered mouth where the rock went through, and it seems clear that some are born to break and some to mend, and all to blossom when we least expect it. I get my old gloves and a broom and begin to gather slivers in the sun. As I pick and brush and sweep the shattered bits of clearness into a pile, they begin to sparkle like a treasure that waits to cut us. Though tired, I feel blessed for where I've been, blessed to know that neither stone nor glass nor copper can satisfy the vastness that holds us. I give thanks that I'm a gatherer not a breaker, at least for today, and hold the rock that the desperate being held, feeling his heat still on the stone. I cover it with my own and toss it back to the earth, for the next being, desperate or peaceful, to hold and use.

STONE OF LIGHT

Something has shifted. One more time. I'm not sure what. But I've given up another inch of making for another inch of being. And though this periodic stripping is disorienting, I'm always more alive once letting go of what needs to be shed. The more I feel, the less I know. As if life is a story that at some moment of softness starts to undo itself, step by step, back to the beginning. The small doe looking for food in our yard lifts its head as if to agree. It's always the same. A lifting that goes nowhere and everywhere. Awake, we struggle to stay awake. In trouble, we try to quiet our pain and fear. It's the most difficult and blessed of careers: perpetually waking. Like a Sisyphus of Wakefulness who rolls a stone of light, we struggle so hard to be here, to stay here.

CIRCLING THE SUN

The homeless man is barking at the taxi honking for him to get out of the way. I see beneath his anger and dirt. He's just tired of calling out to a world that doesn't see him. He pounds his chest. His heart is full of blood like yours and mine. Across the street, this lost kid is floating on meth, his young soul waiting for him to land and start his life. The light changes, but there's nowhere to go. How did we get here, wrapped in the difficulties we wake in? Circle the sun enough and we all lose reasons like gloves in an alley. Everyone we meet is a soft mirror.

EVERYWHERE I TURN

Everywhere I turn people are hurting. When young, I tried to take the hurt away. After feeling my own pain, I tried to quiet the hurt. But now that I've died and am still here, now that I've been stripped of what I thought was so important, the beauty of things shines beneath all that is broken, and I try to listen to the hurt as I would a teacher. Now I see the friction of life as the Universe bending us along, the way wind makes the tops of trees bow and creak. This is different from how we hurt each other, which is often needless—the way those afraid of silence break whatever is near, just to interrupt the silence. Inside, where life rearranges our faults, all we can do is absorb each other's pain, the way earth absorbs rain. All we can do is stay near each other, the way a mother lion swims around her cubs as they learn to stay afloat.

TO RISE FROM NOWHERE

Ise Oluwa is a Nigerian song whose title means "God's work will never be destroyed." Not *our* work that we *claim* is God's, but the work of Existence, Nature, and Spirit that exists before we open our eyes; the work of the Universe that originates outside of our largest dream for each other; the work of Being that carries us without our knowing.

In the Andes, they speak of a shaman who rubs the body of her patients with a candle while singing. Then she lights the candle and reads the flame like an x-ray. How can we touch each other's brokenness and read it like a candle while singing?

How can I say it? Under all our brokenness waits a bottomless spring that rises from nowhere to feed all hearts.

Today I went to see an old man who's forgotten his name. Though everyone is troubled by this, he drifts in a deep joy. The ancient child in him is finally running the show. He was happy to see me and started talking about being a boy crunching through the snow to the barn, then sitting on a cold wooden stool and leaning his head into the loin of a cow while milking it, feeling the heat of the cow blanketing his face. "Now that's something," he said, "That's something!"

BEYOND THE TELLING

I met a woman from Brazil who had to tell her story. Her mother was a difficult woman. But at the piano, she moved like a heron flying low to the water, mirroring the deep. The moment she finished—her hands lifting like slow wings from the keys—her mother was breathless. It was then she seemed to find herself. In that silence between worlds, Clara loved her mother most.

In this world, her mother pushed against everyone. Like a stump too dense to be removed, her mother was always in the way. When someone would ask about her mother, Clara would lean forward and stall, landing in a sigh. It was all beyond the telling: the condescension, the endless criticism, the impatience with everything human, the coldness of her widowhood, the cutting of ties when she began to be shrouded by Alzheimer's.

Yet Clara couldn't let her mother go. She tuned her piano, though she seldom played. But touching what her mother touched made Clara feel close to her. During her last year, her mother sat at the piano, just staring at the keys. Two days before she died, she dropped her thinning hands at middle C and began to coax a song she couldn't finish. She began to fly, then stopped and turned away.

It's been weeks since the funeral, and in her grief Clara keeps searching for the rest of that song. Her therapist says, "Try to let it go." But Clara wants to finish the song so she can begin to fly herself. If she could just finish the song, she might be freed beyond the telling. Every night, Clara feels her best self hover like a note of truth between generations. If she could only finish the song, it might illumine the bottom of her grief. Night after night, she dreams of her mother's hands lifting from the keys like the fingers of a saint.

Listening to the daughter who wants to finish her mother's song, I realize we all are Clara. When I lean in to hug my eighty-seven-year-old mother, I'm trying to feel the young girl that she was, trying to feel and play the one song that shapes us all, though we're so frightened to share it.

All we want is to be freed beyond the telling of what went wrong or how we failed. All we want is to be freed into living the one song that keeps lifting through our hearts. Sometimes I think that what we call coincidence, what we call obstacle, what we call the miracle of surprise—all are notes of the one song bringing us alive, throwing us into each other.

ETERNAL TWO-STEP

What if it's all been misread? What if our insistence on primacy over each other only makes us lonely? What if the clouds we avoid float above our knotted way simply to cry for us, and it's their tears that make everything grow? But all the suffering, you say. All the ways we are so cruel. I have no answer. Only this. The instant our life is conceived, our death is written. The instant a darkness descends, the light that will dissipate it is waiting. The two-step that cradles our lives is unseeable, unstoppable. Like surf that rushes in and undertows out, we are made and unmade. The instant we love or suffer, some aspect of the harmony opens, and what has always been comes together, only to come apart. It renews our fear of dying and stirs our want to live.

STUNG OPEN
FOR A MOMENT

We were visiting friends who summer on a chain of small lakes. Every morning they kayak to a hidden cove. For three years, they've watched a pair of swans nest on the edge of a wetland. Each morning they paddle through the water and drift fairly close, as close as swans will let you. This summer, the female was nesting, the male nowhere to be seen. As they drifted in, they could see the female sitting on her eggs, but her head was underwater, her slim neck bobbing. She didn't move. For three days, the mother swan didn't move. On the fourth day, they drifted closer than they'd ever been to find that she had died. Not a mark on her. With their paddles, they managed to move the dead swan and retrieve a stone-like egg, mottled and heavy, still warm.

They put the egg on the table, and we wondered if the baby was still growing. Had the mother died in bringing this egg into the world? Or had the toxins of our time killed her, and was her unborn already gone? We gathered in the kitchen around the heavy egg. What are we to do with such things, with the stillborn messages of the Universe? The image of the mother swan sitting on her nest with her slender head bobbing underwater seemed to be telling us something. We held the mottled egg to the light. We passed it among us. All the while, the unborn thing was waiting in its heavy shell, a hieroglyph of nature we seldom get to see. We were hushed, as if the eyelid of the Universe had been stung open and we were allowed to climb inside. My friend who found the mother bobbing kept going to the window, looking for something. We felt like some messenger we were counting on had gone missing.

RHYTHM BENEATH
THE RHYTHMS

I'm at the Blue Note in New York City to see Jimmy Heath, the legendary sax player. It's his eightieth birthday. What I find is another kind of music as he gives himself over to a solo in Jimmy Dorsey's "I'm Glad There Is You." His thin fingers press the tarnished keys on his dented alto. The young men in his reed section are watching him with such love that I begin to well up. They're in awe of this spry bundle of energy loving the music out of the night. Jimmy Heath, who in the fifties would go to the library with John Coltrane to listen to Stravinsky, both trying to hear the rhythm beneath the rhythms. When he finishes his solo, the second trombone, a man with graying temples, is so enrapt, he misses his cue. The old master lifts his bony finger and points to him, exhorting, "Yeah!". Then Jimmy brings out Clark Terry, his mentor and friend. A young white kid helps Clark shuffle on stage. It's clear the great trumpeter is confused, and Jimmy holds him before us with such dignity, as if to say with nothing but his smile, "This is not entertainment. This is a life before you." He leans next to his old friend and whispers kindly, "Hey, Clark, remember that tune we used to jig to? Let me hear a few bars." Clark's eyes go wide, and he bursts into a raw cascade of trumpet notes before falling back into his fog. Jimmy touches his elbow softly and turns to us, exhorting, "Yeah!"

THE GIFT
OF DEEPENING

I can't explain or offer conclusions.
Just know that we're surprised into being.
Like divers who open the treasure just
as they're running out of air, we're
forced to let go of what we want
in order to live another day.

The deepest place on Earth is not a physical place, but the stillness we enter at the bottom of our pain, at the bottom of our fear and worry. The stillness we enter there opens us to a spacious state of being that some call joy. When we put down our dreams and maps of memory, precious as they are, we can feel the pulse of life. Then all we could ask for is softly between us, when too tired to deny that there's nowhere else to go. These moments of unfiltered depth are brief. We may only experience a handful of such openings in a lifetime. But like the strong chorus of stars that watch over us, we can navigate our way through the dark by following them. I'm thinking of the time we met in our grief after losing my father and your mother. We found ourselves sitting on the edge of our sorrow like a cliff we couldn't leave or jump from. I'm thinking of the time we felt complete for no reason after falling in the grass with our dog and the light softened all we were carrying. It is these visitations to the deepest place on Earth that make life bearable, that draw who we are more fully into the world, that help us grow softer and stronger at the same time. No one can will these moments to open. No one can find them in the same place twice. And no one can live without them.

TAKE ME DOWN

The gift of deepening is that the heart—that ancient fish—swims closer to the center of the Earth, and the rush of being so close to the fire at the center is indescribable. Such deepening can stop us in mid-speech. Or cause us to drop the soap in the shower. Such deepening can rearrange everything, the way sand on the ocean floor stirs and settles around what no one sees. On days like today, it makes me gasp at the sun warming the horse in my mind till it slips out of its barn. On days like today, I can smell music and hear flowers. And the flower of our pain braids with the music of our love until your story is my story. Until we feel the common ancestor we came from.

Before We Die

They say cicadas spend most of their lives underground, only to emerge in their last phase. In ancient China, a cicada was placed on the tongue of someone dying to emerge the presence of their soul. Why not on the tongue of someone living? Why not place your belief on the tongue of someone you care about so they can emerge before they die?

When loved, we all discover lies, the way we all get caught in rain. But we lose our birthright of presence when we continue the lie after we know it's a lie: when I realize it's someone else's place in line I hold and pretend it's mine, when I know the thing just said is devastating and I keep smiling, when I pretend nothing has changed though everything has changed, when I know the cry in the night is for real and I still roll over, when I know I can confront my mother with her pain at living, but fear to constantly.

I have never feared the future, only in weak moments my ability to reach it. Now, after burning dream after dream to light my way, I wonder when my soul will emerge. I sit in the unknown and wait, which feels both awkward and courageous. And waiting in this way, with as little as possible between my history and my unlived life, I realize all I have to do to stop the lies is to rub my conscience like a cicada till my troubled self goes still as a lake. And below the stilled trouble waits the quiet depth that feeds all souls.

Depth Seeks Us

We met in the mountains, far from the sea. But in his eyes I saw the sea. Somehow we'd known each other for a long time. He was born and raised in Montreal, and his English cupped in French lapped like small waves in the air between us.

On the third day, he said, "I don't tell this very often but I was not very happy as a young man. I worried about the world and if all that mattered would make it through." He looked younger than he was. He folded his napkin and continued, "I was annoyed by everything, never sure if those who put things together could outlast those who break things apart. It made me somewhat dark."

He leaned back, "Everyone thought I was too critical. But we were all trained in the mind at an early age. Anyway, I was twenty-one, half-interested in everything, on a harbor ship full of tourists, annoyed at their eagerness. The clouds were thick, and the sea was choppy. Suddenly, a school of belugas circled the stern and everyone went running. I saw their soft whale heads round through the surface and return, and thought, *How disappointing that this is all we get to see.*"

He sighed and shook his head a bit, "I wandered to the bow to get away from everyone and leaned over the rail. The ship bounced into the waves, bits of spray on my face. It felt good to be left alone. And then from under the bow, a mountain of a fish lifted the ship. It was a great blue whale peeling back the sea. And there—right before me—its gigantic eye staring into mine, an eye as wide as peace, as deep as all time. It stared through the bottom of my heart. I tell you—that moment—eye to eye—felt like a lifetime. And in that brief lifetime, everything was aglow. I can see it all now. The water streaming from its Godlike eye, the God in that massive eye searching for the God in me. And before it swept back into the sea, it took all my doubt with it. Everything seemed softer and truer."

By now, his eyes had widened in the telling and we were drifting into each other even more. He took my hand and said, "I was born in the eye of the whale."

THE OTHER NAME
FOR HEAVEN

It was an image in a dream: of a Buddha statue slowly coming alive, and after a time—which could have been years—it lifted its head as if hearing a bird, and in that instant its heart, which from years of being still was now in its head, dispersed like milkweed blown about by the wind. I was in that half-wakeful state and tried to enter the dream further, when my dog licked my face. She wouldn't let me sleep. I let her out and cleaned her dish. I couldn't stop seeing the Buddha statue, its heart moving into its head after years of coming alive, only to disperse into the world. Is this the other name for Heaven, when devotion to a path ends with us becoming part of the path? Is this the journey I fear and crave?

BEING IN TIME

Lying on my bed in the afternoon, my eyes have been closed for long minutes of nothing. Eventually, the stillness opens and I'm under a drop of slow rain that is rippling on the surface, like when I'd lie on the bottom of the lake as a boy. The drop of clearness goes everywhere as it joins the waves rippling out above me. The fear I carry is such a drop. The love we know is such a drop. Our very lives are such a drop. It's a perfect expression of being in time. All of who we are enters time and ripples through everything, joining the world as if we'd never been. How can I see something like this with my eyes closed while breathing slowly, lying on this bed? What to do with such ancient knowledge? Do I tell the grocer the next time I buy milk? Do I wait and tell Robert the next time we talk on the phone? Or do I simply swallow it sweetly as I ripple into everything?

The Radiant Flow

Let [yourself] look back on life with the question,
"What have you truly loved, what has drawn your soul aloft,
what has mastered it and at the same time blessed it?"
FRIEDRICH NIETZSCHE

Last night I fell into another dream and found myself in an ancient library of light whose books had folded wings for covers. I opened the wings of one such book. The light coming from its pages was so bright I couldn't read the words. Just then a broad-shouldered being appeared and said, "Standing by your core allows you to take in the light." I turned and he smiled. I put the winged book down, admitting, "I have fumbled with so many tasks that have kept me from the light." He said, "I am Ranran." I gasped, "Bashō's famous student?" He knew nothing of his fame. Ranran was the Samurai who resigned to devote himself to poetry. I took his hand, "What made you put down your sword?" He slouched and turned away. I said, "I didn't mean to pry." He came close and stood up tall, "Don't apologize. One of the most intimate things we can do is ask an honest question." I thought to ask again. He sensed this and backed away. I said, "No. Wait." He began to recede into the book I'd put down. He was gone. I picked up the book and opened its wings. Now I could see what was there. On one page was a poet sitting in the grass. On the other, a Samurai, both hands on his sword. They faced each other as mirrors of the same soul. Below the drawing of the poet I found this conversation:

Samurai: *The mind can lead us to the threshold of Wisdom.*

Poet: *But only the heart can Enter.*

Samurai: *The mind weaves meaning like a Spider.*

Poet: *But only the heart can leap into the Stream.*

Samurai: *We are given a mind to navigate Life.*

Poet: *We are given a heart to be Alive.*

A DELICATE CROSSING

I'm thinking of Robert, my oldest friend, seven states away. He understands all of me. There's no translating with Robert. We knew each other the moment we met. That was forty years ago. How will I manage if he should die first? How will I endure the emptiness his going will open in me? He sees, hears, and understands without trying. He's the old soul I've found and lost before. When he goes, he'll pull me into the center, where I will have to befriend the emptiness. Perhaps this is the enduring gift of grief.

THE HISTORY OF MY HEART

It has pumped strong since my first breath. Early on, it grew like a fish, no limbs, no eyes, just swimming in place while I tried to do what I was told. It knew nothing of where I would lead it or where I would be taken. As I grew, it spread into a red bird whose wings stirred me with a want for impossible things. But wanting, falling, loving, dying, and being battered wore me down to life on Earth. Beating in the face of so many abrasions, it only toughened, its cords of muscle eating my heartaches like calisthenics, always whispering in my sleep, "Give me more!"

While struggling with cancer, my heart grew very still. The doctors thought it was going away or back to where it waited while I was being born. It was only gliding beneath the storm. Now on the other side, it has morphed again. How to say it? I've become a mold hollowed by my sufferings: all to be filled by my heart, which has slipped its casing completely, pouring itself into the contours of my being. Now it washes everywhere: behind my eyes, my lips, inside my fingers. Now, wherever you touch me, you touch my heart.

From the Wooden Bridge

I keep watching the one stone over which the stream is singing. What did that stone accept or let go of to be given the privilege of settling just below the surface, so the entire stream could pass thinly, unveiling its shimmer and disclosing its song? How did it know not to rise too far or sink too low? What must we accept or let go of, so that life can reveal its song through us? How do we not rise too far or sink too low? How do we stay immersed in the glorious thick of it?

THE PRACTICE OF
RELATIONSHIP

The beginning of love is to let those we love be perfectly themselves,
and not to twist them to fit our own image. Otherwise we love
only the reflection of ourselves that we find in them.

THOMAS MERTON

I t's so tempting at times to withdraw and watch life
go by, but it's through relationship that we come
alive and heal. There's no other way but to open
the door to our mind, to our heart, and venture out,
knowing we will be changed by everything and everyone we
meet. Yet try as we do, we seldom come close to what we aim
for. I go to love you and miss, hurting your feelings. You aim to
protect yourself and push me away, a little too hard. The friend
we encourage to be herself finally stands up, knocking down
everyone near. Still, our heartfelt attempts, clumsy as they are,
are the seeds that restore the world. All the spiritual traditions
speak about renewal through relationship, and all agree that
God—or the Spirit of the Universe, or the Ultimate Bareness of
Being, or whatever name you want to give to Essence—remains
an indwelling presence until revealed in the world through
relationship. In time, meaning is revealed through relationship.
Of course, we need to be alone and then together. Of course,
we need to retreat and then run into each other's arms. But the
beauty is that the cycle of relationship is never done. And with
each turn of relationship, we are transformed.

The Labyrinth to
Shared Happiness

Though I run to get out of the rain, it's standing in the rain with my hands on my heart that is cleansing. Though I run from the pain, it's standing in the pain with my face to the sky that is healing. So I never stop peeling the hurt, never stop trusting life to burst through whatever I have to face. Even when lost, there's a truth we carry that—when released—can return us to the ground beneath all trouble, beneath all pain, beneath the worm in our mind that wants to run. Facing things together is how we move through the labyrinth of trouble, from thinking alone to feeling together. So when my head is burrowed in what I can't put down, when I can't find what I've just said, please, hold your kindness like a mirror, so I can begin again. Tell me that, hard as it is to accept, the path is right where we are, when too exhausted to chase anything. Remind me that the angels we seek flutter within us, using our hands as their wings.

THE PRIVILEGE OF AWE

It is more important to want to do good
than to know the truth.
PETRARCH

One day Anna goes to the mailbox, surprised to find a two-page letter from her father who lives in the old country, who lost his right hand in the war, who seldom writes because he was right-handed. It undoes her that he should write, not out of emergency but simply of his day in his eighty-ninth year and of the smell of towels warm from the dryer. It causes her to glimpse the young man in his old shell, the one who wanted to bring a child into the world despite the war, because of the war. It makes her hold his letter, with its childlike scrawl, as she would a flower pressed in a book long before she was born. That night, an ocean away, he dreams of his younger self searching for his missing hand.

The following day, when Walter's sisters tell him that his mother's mind is crumbling, he confesses that she's always clear and thoughtful with him. They shoot back, "She's always trying to be her best self for you." He's stopped. They're right. But then he thinks, *How can that be a bad thing, to love someone enough to want to be your best self?*

That night Paulo is describing his grandmother's life to a friend: how she was stolen as a child and brought to this country, how she was raised by strangers and placed in an arranged marriage, how the man she married was an alcoholic. As he says the word alcoholic, he realizes that, though he's told her story many times, he's never seen it through her eyes.

Growing up, he only knew her huge heart. Now that she's gone, he wonders how a huge heart can come from this. He wishes he'd asked for more stories.

And last Thanksgiving Bonnie bought a puppy and named him Amos. He slept with her all winter, curling in the back of her legs. In April, it occurs to her that Amos has never seen spring. Quickly, she drives to the park, his wet nose against the window, unclips his leash, and watches as he sticks his snout in the air. He darts in glee after squirrels hopping in that irregular way. She's softened by his wide stare at birds living in the sky. For the moment, her love of Amos allows her the privilege of awe that lives in the rawness of things.

Now I'm on a plane because they say your heart's enlarged. They call it *cardiomyopathy*. I call it *Flower-Inside-That-Won't-Stop-Opening*. We drive home. I stock the fridge and pick up till there are no more dishes to do. Then we sit and sigh, and you well up, "I'm so tired." I rub your hand. We do this for hours. You start to doze again, and as you drift, you mutter, "Why would you do all this for me?" I gently try to wake you, "Don't you get it? I love you." You're smiling in your sleep. I tuck the blanket close to your neck, careful not to tear the flower you've become.

In Order to Be, Hold

When you stitch me up or calm me down, or the other way around, we slip into a lake that steams the heat off all trouble. Not that we leave the world. Actually, we enter it more completely until what's sharp and hot can be handled. Then our dreams, our obstacles, our detours, where we start, where we land, what's in the way, what helps us along—all of it becomes kindling for a bareness no one can live without and which no one can withstand alone.

THE URGE TO FLY

My whole life, stirred by the urge to fly, unsure, even now, what it means for a heart to fly. Over and over, I try to glimpse what's revealed when we hold nothing back, compelled to merge with what I see. And so, the dream, the ascent, the burning moment of Oneness, the burning up, the fall, the crumbling into ash, the despair, the beginning again. And those of you kind enough to love me along the way, you've known me oddly by the part of the cycle in which you found me: as a dreamer, a rising star, a brief selfless light, as someone burning up, or broken and smoldering, as someone lost, or searching again for what it all means. When clear enough or broken enough, I can see *you* in *your* cycle. Sometimes it takes years, but when we bump into each other at the liquor store or at LensCrafters searching for new frames, we find each other somewhat different or undone. Sometimes—I can tell—you think I'm pretending to be other than I am, when I'm just in a different part of my cycle. Now you think I'm standing too close. I just want to compare notes. I just want to understand how you've turned into a flower or a bird with one wing. As for me, I now think the heart is a red fish gulping its way through a sea of light. But what's this all feel like for you? I confess that I've worn out so many selves, it seems useless to go by any one name. Still, I wouldn't have it any other way. It's left me raw and humbled. I know now that love is the ability to hold someone through all their changes, not too tightly but the way the sky holds the sun. Knowing the unalterable spot beneath our current face is where God first kissed us into being.

Things Get Complicated

For example, the toaster needs to be cleaned, and taking it apart, the last screw loses its thread, and I can't take the bottom off completely or put it back together. But it was my grandmother's toaster, and I'm not ready to get another. But no one will fix it, and I can't figure out how to. So I stop having toast for a month until I can accept it's time to let it go. And somehow, though I feared I'd lose something dear, I strangely feel closer to my grandmother. Because it was never about the toaster.

Relationships are like this. There are times we can't take them apart or put them back together, and we have to live in between until our dreams of relationship lose their thread. Then our sense of worth appears with the sudden realization after loss that we're somehow closer to things anyway.

What I'm trying to say is that moving through the world is inevitably complicated, while being in the world by its nature is simple. When in the midst of complication, we're asked to return to direct living, which means: to say what is true when it is true, and to hold things gently.

THE WISDOM
OF STRANGERS

Everywhere I go, I meet people who've traveled on. Like the young man who grew up outside of Dubai. He now drives a taxi in Seattle and tells me that all roads lead to each other. And the mother of three whose father raised cattle in Nebraska. She now owns an apartment building in Austin. She tells me that when she closes her eyes, the openness of all those acres returns to her. Wherever I go, I listen to their stories until the warmth of being together makes us take off our histories like long winter coats. Then our eyes begin to sigh, and we admit we don't know where we're going, but we love being on the way.

There was the lacrosse coach from Wisconsin who told me that Hemingway said that nobility isn't being superior to others but being superior to your former self. I would say this differently. I've found nobility to be a matter of staying true to the process of erosion that wears away what no longer works. Ultimately, nobility is the moment of grace, however fleeting, when nothing remains between our soul and the rest of life. Everyone longs for this exquisite rawness, though we fear being this naked. Yet after the shock of being so vulnerable, we're empowered by our sensitivity to be of some use. And like the statue of a dog I saw on the Charles Bridge in Prague—that everyone touches as they cross—we shine where we've been touched over the years.

When I listen long enough, everyone starts to reveal their nobility, which has less to do with being superior and more to do with offering the bareness of our being to anyone who needs something solid to lean on.

LOVE IS A GUESS

Buffeted by the wind, a small bird lands on a branch. His landing shakes a bright leaf loose, which drifts to the ground. My dog steps on the leaf while chasing the ball I just threw. The squirrel gnawing at the seed that has fallen from our birdfeeder drops the seed and bounds away when our dog comes close. Any patch of life is emblematic of how interconnected everything is. The sad, oppressed mother of three, so tired after work, leaves fumes of her sadness at the counter in Target. And the cashier has a wave of melancholy on her break that she can't explain. It's astounding that any of us makes it through the day remaining ourselves. Yet if we only remain ourselves, how sad is that? So I want to know you and what has led you to smile when all by yourself. I want to be a student of the thousand moods that shape the human face. I want to meet each soul as a canvas that each day is painting with colors we can't know ahead of time. I touched the grass this morning, and the dew on my palm affirmed that life under all its harshness remains soft. Kindness is love that has no direction, though it needs to come through us to water the world.

POPLARS BY THE RIVER

The poplars are reaching for the sun. The taller of the two leans more toward the river than a year ago. I wonder what they can teach me now that I'm leaning more into the world. I keep struggling to be who I am without shutting out others, and to be with others without giving who I am away. Surely this must be doable. To be who we are *Anywhere. Everywhere.* The poplars lean, as all plants do, toward water and light. But we resist. Overwhelmed or in pain, we turn from the light and push things away, when it's how there is no end to light that is the teacher. There's something reassuring about the poplars leaning. When in grief, I can't bear all the light, though it's the relentless way that light keeps filling dark places that keeps everything possible.

MATEPN

I'm your firstborn. You're eighty-five, I'm sixty. We haven't spoken in fifteen years. Last year, when I came to see Dad, you wouldn't leave and didn't want me in the house. As we drove away, I felt you looking through the curtains. I don't know what you're thinking. Don't know what story you're telling yourself. Don't know in what year, what state, after what pain or sudden fear, you started to burn up, pull in. Don't know when you started to doubt yourself and the world. Or at what point your sadness turned to anger. The other day I was given this photo of you when you were nineteen or twenty, a Russian beauty. You're in a suit with a frilly blouse, your face fresh, your eyes beaming, your hair flowing, your whole life ahead of you. This is years before you imagine me. Since I can't talk to you now, I wonder what talking to you then might have felt like. What if we met in a café while preparing our coffee? What if you dropped your purse and I picked it up and said hello? What if we sat in a corner and looked into each other's eyes with the freshness of first meeting? I think you might have seen my soul. I would have asked what you dream of, what you hope for, what you thought of life at the beginning. I would have told you that *mother* in Russian is *Matepn*. I wouldn't say a word of where your life has taken you. I imagine, after a quiet conversation, I'd look at you for a long time, feeling sad that all your lightness will turn to burden. I imagine once I leave that you take out a mirror and preen a bit. I imagine looking back one last time, whispering to no one, *Matepn, Matepn . . . the best of you was born in me.*

WHAT HOLDS
US UP

As all mountains stand on the ground,
As all trees root in the soil,
As all rivers flow to the sea,
there's a substance under all life
that joins us and holds us up.

When learning how to swim, we feel that we're sinking, and yet we don't. In just this way, there's something that holds us up, a mystical buoyancy under all our problems. Of course, a stone will sink and a heart turned to stone will keep dropping. But not all things sink. So our job is to stay light enough to remain afloat and to trust amid the turbulence that there's some element of being that will sustain us, if we surrender to it. This buoyancy of existence doesn't eliminate the turbulence of the surface where we have to live. But as the air that makes up the sky also fills our lungs, what holds us up is around us and within us. It lifts us when we least expect it, with a wave of being that will carry us, when we're still enough to receive it. Yet living on the surface, we never know what will round our edges or touch us in a way that will stop our chatter. It might be when our eyes meet at the farmer's market in the bright sun. Or after a movie in the parking lot when we realize that we've been looking at the same star. Like roots growing a mile apart in the stream, we're touched by the same current of life, though we may never know each other. Despite our complaints, the friction of the world slows us down till we receive everything. Though we often feel alone, we're never alone. And when we feel a sense of being held, we're coming alive. This is where we're really going, into the embrace of where we are.

LOVE IS AS LOVE DOES

This is the world of Grandma Minnie, the Brooklyn of my youth, full of wonder and windows as far as I could see, out of which countless heads would lean and call for children I didn't really know. Those open windows made me feel we were all connected, made me feel that each living room washed into the next. I'd sit on the cement stoop and watch one drama waft into the street and mix with another two brick houses down and on up to the roof where pigeons would peck at something unseen. I loved that stoop. Grandma would always come out to sit with me. Just when I'd be drifting into all the unknown life, as I felt the street turn to a clear stream that started in some other country, as I was squinting to see where it would lead, Grandma would appear in her apron, her big warm forearms hot from baking. She'd drape me in those arms and smile a smile that seemed to know what I was doing.

All it takes is the snap of a towel in morning light and I can see the lighted alley beside Grandma's brownstone, no more than four feet wide. I played handball for hours up and down that alley. This was where I learned to look at things that everyone else ignored—the light off shards of broken glass, the pale dirt lining the cement cracks, the stiff single leaves somehow clinging to certain bricks above my head. It was here, watching a worm inch toward the street, that I discovered the holiness in empty spaces. It's where I found the secret name of wind, which no one else believed was wind because it funneled through an alley and not across a field.

I loved that alley. It wasn't dangerous to me, or dirty, or enclosing. It was a special world of broken elements that no one wanted—void of people, void of the yells coming from the windows up and down the street. It was a private cave in the middle of everything that no one seemed to see. I spent hours, back to the neighbor's wall, throwing a rubber ball off the bricks below Grandma's kitchen window. I'd watch her move about her stove, hear the clank of pots, and the muted grunt of her lift. Our eyes would meet as she'd lay a pan on her small kitchen table and wipe her big hands on her apron. Those warm bread-potato smells would fill the alley, and she'd smile ever so briefly before closing the oven door. And the little rubber ball would return to me, and I'd hold it like the heart of a country brought across the sea.

DAYBREAK

We were standing on the shore of a lake in early October. We couldn't stop watching the yellow and orange hang brilliantly over the water. The late sun was lapping the underside of all the tired leaves. My good friend Bob sighed and told me of the autumn he drove to Vermont years ago to see old friends.

Up before sunrise, he made his way in the dark and was well into the mountains when a shelf of thick clouds began to lift and the sun inched over the horizon. In that slim opening, as if some mythic god like Thor or Osiris had lifted the plate of the Sky from the plate of the Earth, all the light from the beginning came flooding through. What was there but unseen was suddenly undeniable. What seemed dark and heavy was suddenly brilliant.

Bob felt the light arrive as if each day was beginning the symphony of time. The miracle waiting in life was coming into view. The beauty was so unexpected and overwhelming that he burst into tears and had to pull over. He got out of his car and watched the nameless presence overturn the plate of darkness so the day could find its way.

This is the journey we are all on. Every day, the want for friendship has us make our way in the dark, speeding by everything, aware of nothing until the smallest element of life floods our heart. Then everything is known for the moment, and there's nowhere to go but to pull over in awe of the beauty that is always near.

263 PRINSENGRACHT

I had a remarkable day, which I'll tell you about another time. Tonight I must speak of where I've been and only this. I stood in Anne Frank's hidden room in Amsterdam on the Canal of Princes. It was raining slightly, as if tears were being shed by the gods no one believes in anymore. I stood in her musty room with the windows covered, where she glued pictures of movie stars like Greta Garbo on the wall, along with a drawing by Leonardo. In the next room, the pencil marks where her father measured how tall Anne and her sister, Margot, were. This detail broke my heart, the semblance of life trying to live in the midst of mongrel insanity. As I walked the creaky stairs they climbed every day, terrified of being found, I felt my Jewishness. I know but for a shake and toss of the Universe, I could have been arrested in their place, and Anne or Margot might have been born in my home and writing to you now.

Then there were the thinner stairs to the attic, through which she saw her only daylight, and wind swaying through the top of a tree, which last year had to be taken down, because it was in danger of collapsing on the roof. The city tried to keep some of its seeds. As we are trying to keep the seeds of our sweetness alive by preserving the diary of this thirteen-year-old girl, who died of typhus in Bergen-Belsen in March 1945, one month before the camps were liberated.

As we walked back onto the street along the canal, I stopped in front where they were dragged out of hiding and arrested. I saw the reflection of their home in the water of the canal. It was in their home that Meip Geis, who helped bring them food, found Anne's diary after the SS took them away. This was where her father, Otto, returned after surviving Auschwitz, to sit in the shell of his home and read his daughter's diary. What a fate for this lonely, enduring father? There's a grainy film of him as an old man admitting that he had no idea of his daughter's depth, though they were very close. Otto Frank lived to be ninety-one and died in Basel, Switzerland. What was it like for this man to lose and carry his daughter, knowing intimately the best of us and the worst of us?

We walked several blocks in silence and entered a café, slowly returning to life in our own time. My heart kept beating louder in its Jewish resolve and moan. How can I ever be free of our dark lineage? And she, the bright, lost child who showed more humanity than an entire nation gone mad, is one of six million stories, each as full of dreams and troubles as the next. Yet being a Jew is no different than any other tribe gathered and slaughtered for no reason. The human experiment is both great and barbaric.

I don't know where to put all this. Yet life goes on. The people I was with tonight are kind and gentle. The strangers on the streets in Amsterdam were busy living their lives. There was music and laughter, and dogs were looking up lovingly. I took a long breath, trying to inhale the soft light above the café, wanting to believe that such dark times are behind us. I'm glad to be alive, to have been born six years after the Holocaust. Knowing that from the eye of Eternity, it was only by a squint that the dart of chaos missed me and you and those we love. Still, the truth of this young girl, written in hiding, is enough to light the world.

QUIVERING ANGELS

After we die, we weigh twenty-one grams less. This is the weight of wakefulness, light as seven hummingbirds. Who then are these quivering angels? Certainly, care is one, and wonder is another, and our irrepressible want to be in the light, and our will to live. Then there's our need to hold and be held. And let's leave two unnamed, just to respect the Mystery and to honor how much we'll never know. I like to imagine that when we're born, we arrive weighing twenty-one grams less as well, before we learn how to speak. This difference is the weight of knowledge and voice that we accumulate along the way, that turns into wakefulness if we're blessed, that leaves us when we die, drifting back into the well where all souls break down and merge. It's from this well that another soul bubbles up into yet another person. And so, we carry indelible markings from other lives, inclinations and dispositions that we can't quite name or pin down, except to say that they are intrinsic to who we are. Like my love of the sea and your love of wild grasses. Like my friend George's love of wood and my friend Robert's sudden need to learn fly-fishing. It's the quiver of life that illuminates where we are connected. If you put what matters on a scale, it would weigh less than seven feathers and yet it would somehow balance the heaviness that we carry in our heart.

In Case

At times, it's hardship that opens us, like a shovel splitting wet earth. At times, the light of another filters, like sunlight, through all the blinds we've drawn. And sometimes, like now, I'm softened by the glow of those entangled in the dark. They move about like stars that can't stay still, looking for light everywhere but in themselves. I've done this when in pain, or lost, or after I've hurt someone I love. Last night, I couldn't sleep. So I imagined that my breathing was coming and going through the crack in my heart. This relaxed me. So I closed my eyes and imagined that with each inhalation I was owning my mistakes. And with each exhalation I was sending a drop of mercy to those who are hurting, whether I know them or not. Then everything began to quiet—the noise of my pain, the noise in my mind, the noise of the world remaking itself faster than we can break it. And in that winded spot, I felt the air of love lift me. This is why I thank you when we meet. In case what helps me came from you.

Toward What Is

I slip into the water. It's easy to get lost in the strokes, in the soft parting of the clearness, in the slow breathing that no one hears. But under too long and our lungs begin to burn. Thus the need to break surface. Not to bring our whole face out, just enough for a small gulp of air. Yet above too long and we lose the softness and the clearness and things go cold. I think jazz pianists work like long-distance swimmers. Head under, they part the clearness for a sound they keep chasing. Finding a rhythm, they stroke it over and over till the effort is entrancing. And just when you think there's nothing else to feel, they drop a note or two that pierces your heart. It's the one note that holds everything together. It calls in its many disguises: as a neutron, as a question, as a heart, as the sun. Life is the clear home we swim through. Like water, it keeps parting in its kindness, allowing us to live.

RISING OUT OF HARDSHIP

I always hear what's soft breathing inside what's hard. I think this comes from my great-grandfather's family, who hid from the Nazis in Romania, who slept in cemeteries under the blue night and woke with the stories of the dead, which filled them with resilience.

Just today, I heard a woman who'd been tortured softly play a wooden flute. Though she can't put to rest what was done to her, her softness filled the room, making each of us think of someone who's loved us more than we thought possible. And there was the minister born to blind parents. He said with a tremble that his father saw him better than anyone. And the burly electrician spoke of his colonel in Vietnam taking his dead friend from him when he couldn't put him down. And two states away, the stepdad who never knew his father calls his stepson's father to ask him to stay with them, because he wants his boy to have what he could never find. And just last week I met the nurse who helped me walk after surgery twenty-eight years ago. We cried in each other's arms.

So if you think someone is brave, tell them. For they might feel frightened and small, and you will change their life. If you think someone is beautiful and aglow, tell them. For they might feel dark and lonely, and you will quiet their demons. When you reach to help someone who is stuck, you might free the flight of their soul. And they will return when you least expect, to bring you something from the sky. Never underestimate the strength of your kindness to suture the torn.

A PEBBLE IN THE STREAM

Each storm has, like a navel, a hole in its middle
through which a gull can fly in silence . . .
ANONYMOUS, FOURTEENTH-CENTURY JAPAN

Who uttered this? What led them to it? Were they broken in
some war, left useless as a cart stripped of its wheels? Did they
feel the silence while everyone fought around them? Or were
they tumbling through some grief, trying to swallow the death
of a father or a child? Or did some long acceptance of wind and
rain open their heart like a flower, till they heard the ocean swell
and crash though they were miles away? Or did they actually
see a gull fly out of a storm and mirror it to life? Who did they
cough this up to? Was it a stranger or a friend? Did that person
politely turn away? What then? Did they retreat to scribble it
on some shred of paper? In whose pocket was it found? Or was
it left on the table of a loved one too stubborn to listen? What
matters is passed on this way. Inside every utterance-reduced-
to-a-quote is food from the gods wrapped in a struggle, carried
by someone awakened to life.

Like salt from a wave that's left on shore, there's this residue
we call meaning, which we can bring like a smelling salt to those
battered by the storm. Just yesterday I was in a hospital, trying
to soothe the broken fish flapping on their beds, because I had
been one of them. Not knowing if my survival would be hopeful
or taunting, I felt compelled to offer some small thing. Yesterday
it was the gull. I waited for a break in their pain, waited to be
invited in, and dropped the anonymous knowing between us like
a pebble in the stream. It cleared our agitation for a moment.

Today, I keep thinking of the one, eight hundred years ago, who uttered this. I want he or she to know that what they found in their suffering or joy helps.

MOMENT OF LIFT

I was bearing up under a weight I could no longer see, when the exhalation of something older than all my trouble unfurled my understanding, like a scarf blown out of the hands of someone clutching it. And my mind, floating between preoccupations, was now see-through and weightless. For the first time in months, the grief I'd been obeying went silent. I felt whole in a new way, as if the skin of all I'd been through had grown over all my conclusions. I can't name this other than to say: I have moved through something difficult that has finally opened. All this bearing up and bearing down to be lifted like a scarf on the wind that a child might chase.

NAVIGATING TROUBLE

Let everything happen to you: beauty and terror.
Just keep going. No feeling is final.
RAINER MARIA RILKE

N o one wants to admit it, but moving through trouble is what leads us to joy. As a guitar or violin is hollow in order to make music, we are hollowed by experience. So avoiding trouble is impossible. This doesn't mean we have to seek out suffering or pray to our pain. We simply have to find the resilience to face what we're given and ask for help along the way. From the beginning of time, human beings have tried to get out of here, only to be humbled to find that Heaven waits inside what we wake in. Ultimately, we're asked to navigate trouble, not to seek it or eliminate it. Like beavers, we gather and build a dam in which to live, only to block the flow of life's river. Then trouble comes along to break the dam down, so we can be baptized again in the river. We can't keep each other from this process. We can only hold each other up when the dam breaks and keep each other from drowning when the river of life sweeps us under.

HOW TO EMPTY

First is to see things as they are.
Then to meet things as they are.

This is how it happens. Everything runs smoothly till suddenly the body, like a car, overheats. It coughs and creaks. It won't start in the rain. For me, my stomach was unable to process all I swallowed, and one day it stopped working like a backed-up sink. One too many bites and the pain was unbearable. After a week of tests, I was at the store picking up cottage cheese when I realized I had to keep living. I put on James Taylor. As he sang, I started to cry. Under the song, my heart was widening. When I got home, you called and I broke down. Though now I understand I was emptying myself of all that didn't matter. We start out wanting everything, never imagining how much everything weighs. Then we can't swallow things that eat at our gut. We call this integrity. Then one by one, we're forced to put things down in order to go on. Like a bird dropping food three times its size in order to fly.

GUNS IN THE STREAM

Five years ago, I was driving to a conference with a friend. It was fall, and the leaves were abundantly yellow and red. She told me how sudden drops in temperature make the leaves turn bright before they die. An hour or more into the trip, she told me how her brother, when twenty-eight, water-skied right into shore, turned bright, collapsed, and died. She peered into the rash of color and told me how, without introduction, her twelve-year-old son has taken to water-skiing, how he loves the feel of skimming the surface. She looked through me as I was driving and told me that in the shower, when her boy stretches to scrub his ribs, he looks just like her brother.

That weekend, I met a schoolteacher who was hunting on my father-in-law's land. He came into the kitchen a little after ten. Donald and I were on our third cup of coffee. The schoolteacher was inflamed in a tentative way, unsure if he wanted to shout or whisper. He'd been sitting watch and had dozed when a swift rustle startled him. He cocked, aimed, and there, in his sights, the neighbor's girl—crosshairs slitting her four-year-old head. He almost fired, his body thumping against the tree. He heard her mother call and watched her rush the branches to retrieve the child. He said, "I threw my gun in your stream, and one of your cows started to lick it."

Then, there was the country doctor who, after a rash of patient suicides, heard noises in his chest. Years later, when he died, some of the babies he'd delivered, now in their forties, woke with a start, and the world pulled briefly toward his leaving.

And last night, I suffered my dream of Mother on the bedroom floor, Dad standing over her. They were bemoaning their stillborn. She, wanting another. Dad saying no. I cradled her. She moaned and swayed and changed into her mother. She clutched and cried, then changed into her mother's mother. We were kneeling and rocking in a desert where I was holding my oldest mother who whispered me home. She said, "You must never close down. Or you will vanish."

The One Who
Goes Nowhere

In the Japanese temple, it's quiet and dark. The massive figures are painted wood, hundreds of years old. Three Buddhas in front, all lighted from below. Their faces glow and cast great floating shadows. The central Buddha is sitting, eyes closed, hands softly holding an invisible flute, or so it seems, playing the hymns of the Universe, which cause him to hover above an enormous lotus, which has given up flowering simply to hold him in place. This kind of quiet has no bottom.

The shadow behind the central Buddha opens like the song of a bird too large to have stayed in its body. To either side, more sedate Buddhas, drifting inwardly. One has many heads, the other many legs.

The sidewalls have agitated warriors in armor. One holds a sword, his head aflame. Another raises his fist, smoke rising from his face. Another seems to be counting, though what he's counting appears to be lost. And the last is pointing firmly to the earth.

The longer I sit, the more I feel the Buddhas keeping the warriors at bay, the inner resisting the outer. Then it seems that the warriors are protecting the Buddhas from the world. As I drop into the stare of each, as my heart grows accustomed to the dark, as my mind starts to feel them breathe, I realize *I Am Them*.

I know that sword and fire in my head. I know the raised fist and the smoke that rises from my face. I know too well the counting of things that won't stay put. And I've pointed stubbornly to where I am, unwilling to budge. Rarely, like now, can I still the faces I carry, enough to hear the one who goes nowhere. I will try again.

THE LIFE OF QUESTIONS

Questions offer us a way to dance with life, not to solve it.

Ketut was a great teacher because she claimed to know nothing. Many wanted to work with her. Some would make long journeys in hopes of studying with her, but she disavowed any notion that she accepted students. To those who showed up, she'd simply say, "Let's just walk together for a while and listen."

Three young seekers met in Amsterdam on their way to find her: Gail, a potter from Tucson; Ben, a financial advisor from Dallas; and Jane, a yoga instructor from Portland. Gail said, "I heard she's very quiet." Ben added, "I heard she doesn't take very many students." And Jane worried to herself that she might be stern. They shrugged and laughed and made their way. Their conversation en route was the beginning of their transformation.

A week later, they were sitting with Ketut on a plateau near her small home, which overlooked a meandering river. She began, "You've come a long way to meet yourself."

Ben was eager, "There's so much I want to know."

Ketut replied, "There's a line in the Talmud that reads, 'Why ruin a perfectly good question with an answer?'"

Gail spoke up, "Are there no answers then?"

Ketut went on, "Life unravels the urge to look for an answer. Instead, we're asked to think of questions as teachers to walk with."

Jane voiced her frustration, "But how are we to learn if there are no answers?" Ketut touched her hand, "We're asked to meet questions, not answer them, to give questions away like bread."

This is how their conversations went. The seekers always felt Ketut's absolute sincerity, though her remarks only seemed to open up more questions. Each day they'd meet on the open plateau and watch the river flow and meander.

One morning, Ketut asked, "So what would you like to ask today that I can't answer?"

Gail and Ben shook their heads, but Jane blurted out, "Why ask questions at all?"

Ketut smiled, "Much of my life has been devoted to staying in conversation with the Mystery. As I get older, I long for the courage to stay in conversation with those who've suffered and given of themselves to keep life going."

Jane grew sharp, "But isn't anything simple and direct? Why do we have to keep circling back on what we already know?"

Ketut moved closer, "Because all knowledge is provisional—a snapshot of the flow of life which never stops. Like this river, life keeps shifting as we huddle over our small, fixed picture. So knowledge must be continually revisited. That's why we ask questions. The life of questions is the one art that never fails."

The river of their time together meandered this way for weeks. Ben's intense need to know began to ease, while Jane grew more frustrated, and Gail just liked the sound of Ketut's voice. By now, they were helping with chores and meals. Over dinner one night, Ben asked, "How do we learn from those we don't like?"

Ketut sighed, "I was trapped by this when I was your age. There's an old saying, 'An enemy is a person whose story you haven't heard.' The enemy whose story I needed to hear was my father. Through my struggle with him, I learned two questions that lead us beneath all cause: What have you been through? And how does it make you the way you are? The hard part is getting to a place soft enough to ask."

Jane was so uncomfortable with all this unknowing that she blurted out, "You play the humble master all the time. I don't know what I'm doing here."

Ketut let the silence soften the space between them, then looked at Jane and said, "Eventually, you will go home and realize your struggle is with yourself. When you do, don't feel bad about tonight."

Jane wouldn't look at any of them. Ketut continued, "Like a crack in a wall, your one true question is letting in a trickle of truth, but two of us can break the wall with love and swim in the river of truth. It's the swell of that mysterious water that lets us know each other at all."

Jane began to well up and Ketut said, "The swell of that water is rising in you now." And Jane began to weep. Gail went to comfort her when Ketut motioned her to stop, "Stay near, but let her feel her questions."

The following week, the three young seekers were ready to make their way back into the world. They were more alive but less certain of their path than when they arrived. On the morning of their leaving, they met with Ketut one last time, to voice a quest each would carry in their heart.

Ben began, "I want to learn how I can meet life and not my ideas of life." Gail spoke next, "And I want to know what life is, once I stop waiting for things to happen." Then Jane admitted, "I want to know which of my gifts are still unopened."

Ketut thanked them for caring enough to keep her company for a while. She hugged them one by one and said to each, "You are very wise."

Ben was very tender as he finished telling me this story of his youth. He never saw Gail or Jane or Ketut again. He stared off, "That was so long ago." He seemed about to cry, then said, "The last thing Ketut offered us was that questions are doorways. She started to walk away, then turned and said, 'You must ask a question as you would open a door that you'd like to walk through with another.' And then, she added, 'At least, this has worked for me.'"

LIBERATED BY THE RIVER

She was young, from India. As she poured my coffee, I saw her name tag. It said *Indra*. I asked if she was named after the Hindu lord of rain and thunder. She smiled and nodded, as if her parents gave her this secret to guard her against the roughness of the modern world. We all need the protection of the gods. I have long sought the counsel of Saraswati, the goddess of wisdom and learning who plays a music that's hard to hear. I once thought I saw her inside the hands of a dark and tender folk singer who played deep into the night. And recently, I learned of the god Yu Shi, the Chinese master of rain, who can cleanse a troubled soul of its history. Indra handed me my coffee and offered to lighten it. For a second, I thought I saw her white elephant in the kitchen waiting for her to get off work. I gave her what was in my pockets. No tip enough for this quiet kinship.

SMALL MESSENGERS

The eyes of the snow monkey, neck high in water, are enough to make me believe in reincarnation. They are tender and accepting, as if a hundred sages incarnated behind those eyes. His soft stare jars me from the small perspective I have clung to called my life. Suddenly, I realize that we are small things, whose burdens swell from thinking we are big, sensitive things, whose pain increases for thinking we need to thicken our skin. Oh, God sends small messengers to peel us open. I would laugh if I were not so thoroughly thrown from the horse of all I know. Is what we go through put in our way to reduce us to what we truly are? And what is that? Are we grains of Spirit put here to pollinate each other? Briefly, before life burns up the message, I can see that all my experience—my struggle with identity, with being loved and loving, my struggle with beauty and pain—all of it disrupts my conclusions, like pebbles of light dropped into the lake of my mind.

INSIDE THE DARKNESS

The way stone learns over time to be smooth, I've learned that I can affect change only if I'm willing to be changed; that letting go is more life-giving than holding on; that accepting my death is a threshold to feeling the power of being alive. What I thought made me different is only an illusion I cling to when I pray to the god of significance. Now when feeling less than, I try to return to my alchemy through cancer, the dark flowering teacher that tore the mask of ideas from my face. I've learned over time that what keeps me going is what I share with all living things. I've learned that any storm can be a guide, pushing us to live beyond the shell we didn't know we were polishing. During the storm that makes us drop what we think is important, my ambitions shattered like windows, and I was stunned by the light off all the broken bits of glass. I confess I cut myself trying to piece them back together but finally accepted they were more beautiful in pieces. I put them in a bowl of water and left them in the light.

NAVIGATING TROUBLE

I almost died. It could have gone either way. And as I was jettisoned back into life, I saw something that's hard to put into words. But let me try. You might be working to pick something up. Or put something down. You might be desperate to forget something terrible. Or longing for a love to set you free. Or grieving someone who is irreplaceable. Or trying to find what will keep you going. Fortune or misfortune. Love or loss. Every circumstance incubates the soul so it might germinate while we are here. And wishing you were someone else or somewhere else only makes things worse. I know it's hard to look this deeply into what we're given. But at the cellular level there are even spaces in stone. And spaces of light in everything dark. And spaces of safety in rushes of fear. And spaces of release in flashes of pain. Even spaces of dawn in the cramps of grief. It's not about running from one to the other. But entering where we are—thoroughly—until we can see a way through.

RIGHT-SIZING
OUR PAIN

*For all these years, you've lived under the illusion
that, somehow, you made it because you were tough
enough to overpower the abuse, the hatred, the hard
knocks of life. But really you made it because love is
so powerful that tiny little doses of it are enough to
overcome the pain of the worst thing life can dish out.*

RACHEL REILAND

I t's so human to distort or inflate whatever we go
through, especially when in pain. When under the
thumb of cancer, when everything was alarming and
unpredictable, it was easy for me to see the world as
alarming and unpredictable. But in moments of grace, which
I had no control over, I was humbled to discover that life
was still safe and trustworthy, regardless of what I was going
through. In time, this was a comfort and a resource. And so
I was challenged to right-size my pain, not to inflate it or
minimize it. But to let it be exactly what it was: a transforming
tight space to live through in a vast and expansive Universe.
By our nature, we expand and contract. As I write this, my
lungs are expanding and contracting, and my eyes are dilating
and constricting. And by its nature, pain constricts and love
expands. Understandably, we all want to run from our pain,
and when we can't, we fear we will disintegrate. So an essential

and personal spiritual practice is to continually right-size our pain to exactly the shape and press of what it is—no more, no less. No one asks for pain. Yet like the rhythm of our lungs, which help us breathe, and the rhythm of our eyes, which help us see, the rhythm of our pain, when faced, helps us to be.

DRINKING FROM CENTER

Some say there's a fire at the Center of our Being. How does anyone know? Though I believe it. Sometimes in dream, I go there, and it's not some hell. More like a lake of light that drinking from heals. And healing is not erasing what life does to us. Rather, drinking from Center knits all the scars into a fabric that can't be torn. Regardless of how we get there, no matter what is broken or lost, the weave binds us. We call its pattern beauty.

CÉZANNE IN SNOW

I woke this morning at a loss that it had stopped snowing. I don't know why. I thought of Cézanne in his grey apartment in Paris staring at the apples on the table, not sure where to start, trying to eat them with his eyes. The last few days I've been feeling that old ache that lets me know I'm alive and tethered to everything; feeling that invisible thread floss my heart. Like fishing line tied to a dock, no one's pulling it. It just moves with the ocean when everyone's asleep. The thread of everything tugs and pulls, making us ache for no reason. Though I still search for what makes me feel this way and that. Last night I dreamt I was flipping through the seven hundred channels bouncing off the satellite, and one had all the people I've ever loved behind the screen. They were walking toward me. I could see them up close but couldn't touch them. Then I woke at a loss that it had stopped snowing. I don't know why. I feel like the oak today, leafless in the winter air, glad to be out in the open, ready for something tired to land on me. I wish it would keep snowing. And the sadness in my heart, which is falling like snow, keeps saying, *Be thankful. You're going to wake.* And the sun slipping through the trees stuns me with its assurance, *You are awake.*

Staring into the River

I met a soldier back from Iraq. We wound up having a beer on a cold night in the Midwest when everyone seemed to avoid him because he couldn't hide his pain. Alex was sent overseas through the National Guard, as part of the building corps. He was supposed to be behind the lines, building makeshift roads and temporary bridges, setting up transformers and portable camps. Of course, war doesn't honor such boundaries.

He has one dream that keeps recurring, of an Iraqi woman he refused to help. On what began as an ordinary day, Alex, Fred, and Earl were sent to survey a site on the other side of a town being taken. They were along for the ride when the squad was shot at. They pulled over and began to flush out any remaining insurgents. It was the first time Alex saw live fire. The soldiers swarmed, door to door, forcing family after family into the street. As they left the fifth home, the soldier next to him was suddenly down from a bullet in his shoulder. No one could tell where it came from. Guns were firing everywhere.

The sergeant grabbed a young local woman. She broke away and ran to Alex. The sergeant went to grab her back. Alex reflexively protected her. The sergeant grabbed her and threw her back in the open, then shot her in both legs as an example. She was writhing in the street. Alex was now on the ground beside the Jeep, his heart screeching like a siren. Through the undercarriage of the Jeep, their eyes met briefly. Then he heard an anguished cry. Earl had been shot and was bleeding on the ground. Alex shimmied under the Jeep and, through the dust, he watched the sergeant burst a flamethrower up and down the length of the young woman. When it all settled, a corporal was dead, and Earl and another soldier were injured.

But he couldn't take his eyes off the young woman smoldering in the street.

Alex was broken, unsure how all this happened. Now back in the States, she comes to him every night in this dream. Nameless and beautiful, she runs past the sergeant, beckoning for Alex to save her. She removes her veil like a lover but always bursts into flames when he touches her.

I listened to Alex for much of the night but finally had to go. As I started my car, I knew he would never recover. That night, I dreamt of the young Iraqi woman on fire leading Alex and me to a dark place near a river where a Rwandan Hutu soldier couldn't stop feeling the clutch of a Tutsi woman he'd raped and killed. Next to him was an Afrikaner guard who couldn't stop feeling the welts of a particular prisoner he'd beaten on Robben Island. Somehow the welts he'd inflicted were now all over his pale, white body. The four of us sat staring into the river, unsure how to rid ourselves of the horrors we'd taken part in. I kept wanting to say, "Not Me!" But somehow I felt just as responsible.

Now part of Alex's pain lives in me. Now I've become a blood cell rushing to the site of the injury, though I don't know what to do. Now I wake with this recurring thought: What would we have to water—within us and between us—to grow something holy enough that would keep us from hurting each other?

BEYOND MYSELF

You ask why such things happen, why hearts break, and why we hurt each other. I don't know. And anyone who says they know is pretending in order to avoid the tidal wave of Mystery that surrounds us. We are cast about as soon as we wake, every day, and this unpredictable surge, this sweep as soon as we enter the street, is something we crave and fear. I only know that this surge is sometimes disguised as surprise, and sometimes it covers us with a veil we call sadness. Now leaves are falling and someone is playing Brahms in the park, and the surge is rising in my throat to meet the music mixing with the leaves. I only know that this surge keeps reaching through me, as it has since the beginning. And that asking why never brings us closer. Now I'm coated with a thousand acts of care that began in difficulties that took place before I was born. Such nameless care comes through when we don't rush to close. How I unfurl when my heart aches beyond myself. As in this moment, wondering if all that we feel is music just waiting for hands to play it.

IN A UNIVERSE
THAT BREATHES

The stars this January night throb in place the way we on Earth shimmer below our trouble. Everyone I pass shows this shimmer: the waitress at Brewster's, the attendant at Citgo. Even the couple arguing at the light: their shimmer throbs below their ache, though they think it's gone. And in this snowy field, the stars pulse as if they and we are cells in a Universe that breathes. I held our dog in the crook of my arm this afternoon. As she fell asleep, I stroked her face; her blonde lashes full of a peace I'll never know. Then, on the way here, the sun kept thawing the snow along 131. And earlier, you sipping your coffee, catching me watching you. Moments like these help soothe the small violence we do when we turn away from someone in pain or demean experiences other than our own. God, these stars tonight, I feel them mirror the galaxy inside where we dream of each other. I met a woman from Sarajevo last week who told me that under siege there was no electricity or heat for weeks. Families began to burn their furniture, their clothes, their books—all to keep warm. At first, I felt the crisis of it all. But tonight under these stars that outlast us, can there be any more loving end than to burn what we have to keep each other warm? I throb in place below the trouble of the world.

ETCHED

We are so forgetful that only pain makes us remember. Yet here
is a scar on my wrist, and I can't recall how I got it. Am I
getting old or is this the miracle of healing? We've been told
that scars are ugly. I think they're beautiful traces of how we're
touched by life. To have no blemish means we've fallen through
time with no meeting. What's the point? To die unchanged is
to be an arrow that never lands.

OVER MANY MONTHS

After ten years of swimming, I stopped when Eleanor died. She was one of several dear ones who had left the Earth. There was too much to tend, and part of my heart had stopped, unsure how to continue. Everyone called it grief, but below the name, I felt that the fire in my center was beginning to smoke. I kept my appointments and did the endless tasks, but some part of me felt hollow.

Slowly, over many months, I began to feel the presence of those I lost in simple things: in the sudden sweep of tall grasses, as if Eleanor were whispering something I couldn't quite hear; in the light on a pigeon in Washington Square Park while someone played a saxophone, as if my father were smiling on a bench just out of view; and in the closed eyes of our new dog Zuzu while asleep, as if our dead, beloved dog Mira were slipping inside her to tell us she was near.

Then, one day in summer—after I had told their stories to everyone, after I had called to them so many times that my thread of grief joined the braid of silence that hoists the sun up every day—on one sunny day, I sadly gathered my swim gear and went to the pool. And as I slipped into the water, as I began to glide through that familiar depth, I started to cry, water meeting water. I felt myself enter my body again and realized I hadn't wanted to swim because returning to my life, doing what I always did, would mean that these precious beings that I so love would truly be gone. Gone, as if never here. With each lap, I began to accept both their presence and disappearance, and stroke after stroke, the smoke in my heart began to clear. I kept moving through the water, which kindly parted for me, only to join behind me, as if *I* had never been here. And I could see that life parts for us all in this way. But now it seemed gentle and full of a quiet beauty.

As I left the health club, the wind was lifting the tall grasses in the field beyond the parking lot, and I could feel it circle the earth, bowing and lifting the many trees and leaves along the way, sweeping pollen and spores from field to flower. I smiled in my sadness to feel the voices of time bow and lift me on the edge of the parking lot. And for a long moment, I could feel the presence of those who've come before sweep through me, lifting me into something so much more than me, only to settle me more deeply into life.

NEAR THE CENTER

It was in the Plaça Catalunya in Barcelona. I saw a young woman open her hands as if cupped for water. They were filled with seed, and pigeons flocked to her—in her palms, on her arms, on her shoulders. She threw her head back and laughed. It broke me to realize that, for all our want and fear and will, this is how we embody what is real and make our peace with God. If brave enough or broken enough, we stand in the open cupping our heart, full of its dreams and sufferings, full of loves gone right and wrong, and we wait for a large winged thing to drop from the sky to take it all away. It was then I understood: our dreams and sufferings feed the gods who free us to love again.

SHEDDING
OUR MASKS

*If you're the same person at fifty that you were at twenty,
you've wasted thirty years.*

MUHAMMAD ALI

From the beginning, the problem with masks has been that while they're intended to protect us, they also suffocate who we are. This is akin to the ageless problem with walls, that they wall in as much as they wall out. Understandably, the harshness of experience makes us put on coverings, as thin as veils and as thick as armor, in hopes that these coverings will protect us from the suddenness of life. And any mask will do this for a while before it traps us behind its features. As a sensitive boy in an insensitive home, my first mask was to be stoic when I was hurt, never showing what I was really feeling. This is a common mask. In time, it became a callous between my heart and the world. Deeply thankful to be here after cancer, I was forced to remove that mask so I could once again be touched and surprised by life. Ultimately, masks are temporary Band-Aids until we find a way to trust our native gifts. So we will all put on masks. It's part of being human. The work is to take them off, once we've learned to be strong enough to trust who we are.

WHAT THE WORLD ASKS

Only suffering can break us of the cult of specialness. Only that invisible hand can pry us from our preferences. No need to seek such breakage. Or praise it. Or make a god of it. And no way to avoid it. Just admit when alone that the Atlas in your mind is tired and wants to rest. I was out early toward the end of winter when I came upon a small maple encased in ice. The sun was licking the day. It made the thin tree glisten, and slowly its casing thawed and the maple continued to grow. I could almost hear it gasp to be alive again. I want to welcome experience like that.

PERKS

Contrary to our cartoon of evil, hell has good lunches and many perks that make us think it isn't hell. I've always fooled myself by making what I want look like what I need. There's a difference between telling our story till it unravels to center and changing our part with each telling. When anxious, we reframe everything, like a painter who can't stop touching up his canvas until reality is unrecognizable. And I admit, it's hard not to be distracted by the one who flicks open his lighter offering you a cigarette, though you don't even smoke. Hard to stand before your life like a sumi master and simply brush the one stroke that is essential without revision.

An Early Mirror

While Eisenhower was president, three small, bronze disks were found in China. They are the earliest remnants of mirrors we have. One dates to about 770 BC (in the Western Zhou Dynasty) and was found in a tomb near the Yellow River. Round and rimless, the small looking glass is sided by the profile of two tigers with a wild horse above and a bird below. It's not clear how these early mirrors were made or why. Was the ability to see ourselves discovered by accident? Was a small piece of bronze worn smooth by one too many storms then found? Or was the need to see ourselves awakened by the storm of being human, until some piece of metal was stubbornly rubbed clear? And who decided to frame this early mirror? Why tigers, a wild horse, and a bird? What were they trying to say? In some ways, history has been the tension between clearly seeing ourselves and clearly seeing everything that is not us. Perhaps the maker of this looking glass was wise to frame our reflection with animals. Perhaps they were saying: Don't get drunk on your own reflection. Don't fall in. And never forget the things that pounce, that run, that fly. Perhaps they were saying: If you must look at yourself, protect your soul from self-absorption by holding on to nature.

THE DETAILS CHANGE

Strolling in summer down Bleecker near Broadway, we pass a young Hispanic couple sitting on the curb. They begin to argue. He blurts out, "How can you say that?" She looks hurt. They start squabbling in Spanish. We laugh at them and at ourselves. It's the same argument since the beginning of time skipping between us. The details change. The language evolves. We long to be close, then bump into each other, and tumble through life the best we can. How to stay close without losing who we are? How not to run away or retreat into isolation when misunderstood? How to stay connected and tethered to the truth that outlasts all argument? The next morning, I land on a bench in Union Square where the homeless sleep in the sun this time of year. A damaged man in a T-shirt is walking in circles, talking on a cell phone, though there doesn't seem to be anyone on the other end. A young woman who's listening to music is watching him too. We catch each other's eye, not sure if we should get involved. But that's the mask we all need to put down, the one that keeps us at a distance. For we're already involved. The question is how?

GETTING WIND OF IT

He was so calm and wise, such a sage, that it was hard to believe he was ever a colonel in a war. It was a lifetime ago. It was a rough skin he'd shed. Getting wind of it, the young men at the detention center began to pester him for details. Their noise brought him back to unspeakable moments. The buzz grew so great that he finally stopped one day while rinsing the dishes. Later, he confided that he needed to speak of it, finally, in order to puncture their dreamy notions of violence.

"I began afraid, but when forced, I started cutting and slicing others, and with each cut, I became disemboweled of my want to stay alive." The young ones inched closer. He leaned into the most wide-eyed of the lot, "In the end, all our uniforms were torn, all the flags were burned, and it was no longer possible to discern sides. In the end, I was trying to piece arms to chests just to stop the screaming."

This wasn't what they wanted to hear. The glare of honor and cause was wearing down. Someone asked about patriotism. He sat on a large stone and stared into the empty center, "These are hard truths. You can live without arms, because though we want so badly to touch, it is being touched that heals. And you can go on without legs, because though we dream of seeing the world, it is being still that opens up Eternity."

By now, most were staring into the center with him, and the youngest was quivering with a proper fear. But the strong-willed boy was resisting it all, telling himself that only the weak wind up on the heap. The sage sensed his pride and sat beside him, lowering his voice, "But you can't live without a gut." He poked the strong boy in the stomach, "Because we must digest and break things down." He put his hand firmly on the strong boy's chest, "And you can't live without lungs, because no one has ever survived without a way to take things in." He then leaned close and tapped the strong boy's head, "And you can't live without a head, because we're dead the moment we no longer perceive."

There were a thousand questions but no more words. He stood and walked back into his life. Once again, he seemed sweet. He dropped his shoulders and touched his heart, saying to no one, "Like stubborn fish, we fight the current."

CÔTÔ

I dreamt that I and someone close were searching through a found book. It was old, and patches of each page had faded, enough that the text didn't make sense. We sat near the edge of a sea, and as the wind would gust, the clouds would clear, and in the light, the missing words began to appear. I closed the book so we could talk. When I opened it, the same passages had faded. But in the light, the missing words returned. As I woke, one word stayed with me, *Côtô*. I've searched but there is no such word. So here it is, another metaphor, come from who knows where. For don't we need to stay in the light for the meaning, already written in our heart, to appear? Isn't this why we live in the open? When closed, don't the meanings start to vanish? Not for good, thank God, but only till we come out of hiding. This opening and closing like an old book is the closest we come to freeing the truth. And each time we expose ourselves to light, we reveal another page inscribed in our heart. I'm drawn to call this process *Côtô*.

In the Winter Cabin

My footprints in getting here are filling with snow. The fire is dying down. The paper in this journal is made from the bark of a Lokta tree that grew in the foothills of the Himalayas. The veins of its pulp are visible in the page. Some days, I feel so overrun by the world that I long to be a piece of bark stripped for others to write on. Though hardships cover us, the path of individuation, of meeting life until we are who we are everywhere, requires us to shake off falsehoods and illusions. We have all we need within us. My thoughts now flutter like leaves in some ancient wind I've always known. Outside, the wind is blowing clumps of snow from the branches, and a snow-covered feeder sways twenty feet from this window. I want to shake off all my doubts like snow. My life to this hour is waiting to be uncovered, so I can be touched completely by life. I vow to stay uncovered, longer this time.

GIVING WAY

There are those who cackle like crows to hear themselves speak. They fear they'll disappear unless they hear their voices bouncing off of everything. I know. I was one of them. And those who repeat themselves because they fear they'll never be heard. Like waves they reach farther and farther onto shore. They want to be accepted by everyone. I was one of them too. Now quiet and smooth, through no wisdom of my own, it's hard not to feel for everyone. We simply want to be seen and heard. And in time we trip into what we dislike and fear. This is the apprenticeship of compassion, to open our care to all things, including the darker moods we show no one. Now there's so much truth in every direction that when my heart breaks surface like a diver short of air, all I can do is gasp, *thank you*. The dream of being heard has given way to listening. Like a cliff worn of its broken tooth after a hundred years of wind.

THE REACH
OF KINDNESS

Kindness can accomplish much. As the sun makes ice melt,
kindness causes misunderstanding, mistrust,
and hostility to evaporate.

ALBERT SCHWEITZER

indness is the antidote to everything. Just as water soothes fire, kindness calms how we burn each other from time to time. And under all the ways we burn and hurt, there's the soft and lasting presence we were born with, waiting to blossom in the midst of any trouble. For despite the many ways we try and the many ways we miss, we are kind nonetheless. Inevitably, we're required to step out of the house, afraid as we are of all we might meet. Because it's the kindness and wisdom we will encounter beyond our fear that brings us together, that brings us alive. The truth is that kindness turns fire into light and presence turns misses into surprises. The first reward for kindness is a thoroughness of being. The next reward for kindness is a greater integrity in our relationships. But the most enduring reward for kindness is our experience of Oneness. For being kind renews our kinship with all things.

THE SWIFT ONE

We each live in a home. Some are small. Some are large. Some are kept up. Others are run down. In hut or mansion, we have to come out. For food. To have our body repaired. To make our mechanical animals purr. But sometimes we're drawn out. Into the light. To feel a breeze. To feel the rain. To meet a friend. To rub our face in snow. Sometimes we leave our small shelter because we hear others in need. You could be folding laundry when a sudden warmth in your chest makes you feel uneasy, like when you realize you left the stove on. But you didn't. And so you wonder if you're sensing some need in the world. You dress, do the errands, and all day your heart is on the look for who you're supposed to help. When drawn out this way, the swift one appears in us, and we are for a time stronger than we are, the way seas lift dolphins. Our sense of self is a home as well. Some are small. Some are large. Some are kept up. Others are run down. Whether insecure or full of ourselves, we have to come out. Not to escape our problems or to tunnel through them, but to enlarge the home we live in. And when we dare to give, the swift one appears to help us cross the ocean of suffering.

SMALL LIGHT
AND TIMELESS LIGHT

Everything is lighted, including us.
In the beginning, this is clear.

After the rain, we tip our face to the sun, and our small light is renewed by the timeless light. In relationship, we tip our face to each other and illuminate the one we look at. To illuminate another is to behold them, to show them their light. Sometimes, we struggle so hard to be seen and heard that we empower those who behold us as keepers of our light. Then, we can become so desperate to stay within our lover's gaze that we stop opening our face to everything timeless. Now the inversion has taken place: we have entrusted our light to others.

Spiraling away from our worth, we can become so removed from ourselves that we can court violence as a desperate way to feel. Of course, we are all desperate at times to feel, and we all struggle to know our worth. And we all take turns lifting each other's face back into the sun, reminding each other that we are enough as we are. This is the power of kindness, to return us to our own experience of light and worth.

No one knows why some of us lose our way and some of us find it. The slip from finding our worth to losing it is common. I have given my light away more than once. And I have also been dark, unable to find the light. And I have taken my turn lifting the face of someone bewildered. What's most important is the honest touch that breaks our trance.

Of Course You Can Come

When Ellen's husband passed away, she received a call while preparing for the funeral. It was an old woman living three hundred miles away who asked if she could attend the service. Ellen was taken aback by how far her husband's life had reached. She said, "Of course you can come, but please, tell me, how did you know Sam?"

The old woman spoke with a tremble through a thick Yiddish accent, "I read in his obituary that he was one of the first three soldiers to liberate Dachau at the end of the war." There was a long pause, "I was a little girl then, weighing only twenty-eight pounds, naked and limping. I was shot in the foot for taking a drink of water." There was another pause, "When those soldiers entered the camp, we didn't know if life was ending or beginning. And seeing us, naked and starving, they took off their shirts and covered us." They both fell into a deep silence. The old woman said softly, "I always wanted to thank them but never knew who they were." And so the little girl from Dachau drove three hundred miles to stand at the dead soldier's grave and embrace his widow.

How are we to understand a story like this? Does it tell us that acts of kindness and the gratitude they engender outlast decades and oceans and continents? Does it tell us that kindness like the song of a hungry bird will be answered long after the bird has died? Does it tell us that the smallest effort to restore dignity can save a soul from degradation? Like the one bead of light, after weeks of light, that causes a tulip to finally open, the bead of kindness that is compelled from us, despite our hesitation, will open more things than we may ever know.

PUTTING DOWN OUR BROOM

At seventy-six, my friend Don has the innocence of a child and the wisdom of a sage. He's an accomplished painter and a wonderful teacher. The older he gets, the more I watch him play with the colors of awareness in the canvas of his life. The other day, he said, "I was sweeping my porch when my neighbor came out to cut his lawn. Now, I've always thought he's an asshole. But sweeping the porch, it occurred to me that I might be a prisoner of my own story. I mean, because I see him this way, everything he does will only confirm my story. And that will only bring the asshole out in me!"

So Don immediately put down his broom and waved to his neighbor, shouting, "Hey, what's up?" His neighbor stopped mowing and folded his arms. Don kept smiling and waved again. Finally, his neighbor called him over, and they began to talk for the first time in years. They chatted for a while, and his neighbor said, "You've never seen my house, have you?"

And so, like the farmer who fed the stranger, or the seamstress who hid the fugitive, or the young man who helped the dizzy woman back to her car, another story began.

NATURAL

To say there's a moral order to the Universe is to speak of physics as if it were nature and not our understanding of how nature works. It's how we fool ourselves into believing we are the architects of this journey. But this is real knowledge: while thousands were forced to march barefoot from the concentration camp and shot for slowing down, an old Jew stumbled and fell, and the others being prodded fell on top of him without thinking, because they knew if singled out, he would be killed.

We have this impulse to protect what falls, to bring water to the thirsty, to love what is hurting. Even today, at the food mart, a woman struggles at a pay phone, and I fumble without thinking, "Here, use my cell."

Before we learn to judge and hesitate, we break surface like whales looking for each other. It's not moral. It's natural. I know a vet who lost a leg. Now he rescues homeless dogs. I know a psychologist who stopped seeing clients because he was drowning in their stories. Now he's a painter who gives portraits to the dying.

Each day reduces us to this question: What does it mean to be alive? And each time we reach out to others without thinking, we're given an answer that offers us a little peace before slipping like water through our hands.

On the way home, I fall on the ice while fiddling with my groceries. Two young boys are there in a flash: gathering what broke, cleaning what didn't, helping me up.

IN THE SEA OF DREAM

In the middle of the night, your hand was sticking up from under your pillow—so still and open—as when we finally stop reaching and are just beginning to receive. I gently twined my fingers in yours. You were so asleep, and yet you took my hand. That's how deep we can go. We hold on, even when drifting in the sea of dream. I couldn't see your face, only your hand. And with no distractions, with no dishes to wash or bills to pay, I was winded by all the things you've held and cared for, including me. This was the hand that stroked your mother's face before she died, the hand that cupped a baby bird till it could fly, the hand that cupped my face when I was so alone in my pain, the hand that learned to give our beloved dog Mira shots to ease her arthritis, the hand that sometimes doesn't know how to care for itself, the hand that renews itself nonetheless by planting things in the earth. I wanted to place your hand, like a salve, on my heart but didn't want to wake you. Then your fingers went limp, as if the dream you were falling through was coming to an end. In that moment, I feared this is what it would be like if you were to die in your sleep. I quickly squeezed your palm, and you stirred. I held you and whispered, "Everything's alright. Go back to sleep." And you turned over. It was then I put my head on your shoulder, leaning on the mystery of your heart, of my heart, of the one indivisible heart, as thousands have done throughout time.

AND SO IT GOES

We were walking near the water when you saw something in the waves that I couldn't see. It made the years peel away from your heart. And there, by the sea, the flower of your life opened, and the seed of the Universe you carry, which some call God, was shining like a diamond softened by time. You turned and said, "We have loved each other well. Please, take it." Your wild kindness opened the flower of my life where the seed of the Universe that I carry fluttered out of me like a red bird born to make a nest for diamonds softened by time. So my gift took your gift and flew off to seed the future, revealing something deeper in each of us. And arm in arm, we thanked all that is and happily began again.

The Symmetry of Kindness

The train slammed into the station, injuring hundreds. The engineer was critically hurt. People toppled over each other, bouncing across seats and against windows. There was blood and glass everywhere. One woman shimmied her way to the platform when part of the station ceiling fell, pinning her. She thought she would die. Then the hands of fellow passengers lifted her, one to another, and she was saved. Later, she wanted to say thank you but didn't know who to thank. Once on the mend, she retrieved a list of those who were with her that day. Now, one by one, she looks them up, asking if they had helped her. Each of them smiles and says no. Once with them, she can see what each needs, and so she helps them along. She unpacks groceries for an old woman, listens to a widower's story, and gives a single mom her umbrella. This has gone on for weeks. She keeps trying to find those who helped her, only to help those she finds. Finally, it occurs to her that this is God's symmetry of kindness. She will never know who helped her, so she can thank and help everyone she meets along the way.

THE RADIANCE
IN ALL THINGS

God does not die on the day when we cease to
believe in a personal deity, but we die on the day
when our lives cease to be illumined by the steady
radiance of a wonder, which is beyond all reason.
DAG HAMMARSKJÖLD

J ust as physicists describe gravity as the pull of all things back to the Earth, mystics describe the radiance in all things as the emanation of a presence that brightens everything into being. There are many names for this dynamic. But life as we know it is where the radiance of being meets the gravity of the world. Where inner meets outer, we spark. This is why, in the rubble of Warsaw after World War II, the great Polish poet Czeslaw Milosz could render a semblance of light coming through the devastation. This is why when seeing a boy hung in Auschwitz and asked by another inmate, "Where is God?" Elie Wiesel grimly and mysteriously answered, "In the boy hanging." This is why it takes only one twitching cell in a sea of dead cells to regenerate life, and one seed of dream in a dead soul to bring us back alive. There is a radiance in all things that is indestructible and almost unperceivable. How do I know this? I can't really say, except that I have died and come alive again, through no wisdom or effort of my own. The only explanation can be that the cinder of radiance under all my rubble wouldn't go out. I could have died, and the radiance would have skipped to some other life form. But I was blessed, for now, to catch the light and breathe again.

FLOW OF LIGHT

I was swimming in an indoor pool when the wind outside parted the clouds, and the sun—light-years away—burst through the weightless dark, past other planets, through the bell jar we call the atmosphere, through the mystery of gravity, through the wall of glass that encloses this pool, to spray its light softly through the water, leaving threads of gold dancing on the bottom, which patterned through my mask and on through my eye, to warm the cold spot in my heart. It made me surface and look to the sky, the way primordial amphibians must have broken through the mud. Oh, to realize that light will move through anything transparent. To stay transparent so the gift can move among the living. To know this is our job. I went back under, treading slowly over the dense tile bottom, to be with the shimmer as long as I could.

GRACE NOTES

I learned to play piano at the age of forty-one. I worked my fingers long enough that the uncanny dimension of being played, that all pianists know, appeared briefly. In those moments, beyond all logic, my hands started to behave more quickly than my mind, which was trying to read the notes and position my fingers. My teacher noticed this and thought I was ready to tackle my first piece by Bach, a minuet from a collection he created for his wife, a book she herself copied, known as Bach's *Notebook for Anna Magdalena*.

In the eighth measure of that minuet, there appears a note smaller than the rest. Almost ghostlike, it hovers very near the others like a barely seeable angel or a hummingbird whose path is more readily seen than its body. It surprised me. My teacher called it a grace note—a note that though played and heard takes up no time, a note that matters, though it is timeless. And therein lies its grace.

Now, twenty years later, I realize this is another way to understand the paradox of epiphany, of moments that open and transcend their sense of ordinary time. In truth, every glimpse of Eternity I've ever encountered has been a grace note that has affected how I see and hear, though it's taken up no time in the measure of my struggle. I find over and over that the instant we're washed open by the swell of the Universe is such a note of grace. And the wisdom of mystics and sages reverberates in the timeless space their presence holds open.

When these moments occur, when the mind is touched by something larger than its ability to understand, when the heart is moved by something deeper than its capacity to dive, when the impulse to speak is stirred by the presence of something that can't be named, things happen that defy the boundaries of time. Such moments confirm that we're part of a Unity that's always present but seldom clear, and to be touched by that presence changes our lives.

Moments like the moon, full and stark, rising over the garage between the oak and the maple in the backyard of a friend as we barbecue. Suddenly, the moon is calling in its white silence, drawing the smoke and fragrance out of the meat into the sky, and we, without a word, feel coated with a film of light from another world, the same as cavemen preparing their game at the mouth of their cave.

Moments like the morning of my annual CAT scan on the other side of cancer. When I realize that in the tenderness of being torn open by life, we're like these small, red birds splashing themselves with water as the sun comes up, hoping we will heal without sealing our heart over.

Moments like watching my friend's twenty-year-old cat adjust to being blind. All at once, the cat trying to make its way feels like our sense of being lost no matter how we fill our calendars.

Moments of soft, relentless grace like the other night, celebrating one of our birthdays, the cake on the table, the lights off, all of us caught watching the sparkler on the cake, each of us peering from our own personal seat of darkness, gathering as we do, fixed by the hiss of light flaring between us, feeling the sparks fly, afraid one might burn us, hoping that it does.

Blood of the Sun

Shamans believe that the fire at the center of the Earth, which no one has seen, is a flare of the beginning that never went out. And the energy of that fire shimmers today through the basalt and granite, all the way to the surface where it makes thin trees sway, even when there is no wind. You have to be very still to see this. In winter, you can go far into the woods, take your gloves off, and press your palms to the trunk of an old pine. After the chill parts, you might feel a small warmth of the beginning move up through the tree, into your hands. This will only happen if you believe that music rises from the Earth. This happened to a quiet composer I know. He wasn't sure at first but kept his gloves off the whole way home, went straight to the piano, and began to play. For two days, the flare from the beginning warmed his piano. He kept returning to this music. He played it for his wife and then a few friends. All were drawn to touch their hearts and sway. At the same time, a healer in India was teaching an apprentice how to touch the ill, how to press her palms to the flank of a tired body until she could feel a small flare from the beginning move through her hands to warm the ill one's heart. During the next year, the healer and the composer will dream of each other.

WE'RE INTIMATE NOW

It's early March, the snow almost gone. The old rugged oak in our yard is leafless. It happens that the sun is rising behind its trunk. It slips between its upper fork, the light splitting in every direction. In this moment, the old tree seems to be crucified on the dawn of another spring. The light, spilling through the tree, blinds me as it illumines the world. As I start to see again, I think of Leonardo's drawing of man, arms and legs spread with our small heart spinning in the center, waiting for life to reach it. Maybe this is how it works. Sooner or later, we must spread ourselves to life, naked, mouths open, our hearts spinning in the center waiting for light. The sun has risen to warm the rest of the world, and the tree has settled back into being a leafless tree. The early light has come and gone off my face, and I've settled back into ordinary perception. But we have been lighted. The oak will never be the same. We're intimate now. And there, a fox trots slowly behind the tree. He stops and looks up at me, as if he knows, then disappears.

THE THING FALLING

I walk seven blocks down Pennsylvania Ave. and wander into
this small bistro. Sitting near the bar, I watch all the quiet
strangers being brought water. We're always being watered.
The piano man waits a long while, and when he begins, I feel
something vital stretch in each of us, like roots aching for rain.
I close my eyes and it's yesterday. I was eating a sandwich on a
bench when three birds ducked around branches lifted by the
wind, the way I sometimes catch the thing falling and let it rest
on the ground.

After a while, the piano parts my tiredness like a veil and
I feel possible again. Now I don't know whether to put my
glasses on or keep them off, whether to bring things into focus
or let them come apart. Either way, the sky is calling behind its
clouds, like the stars of truth that burn behind our thoughts.
Each time I get up and begin again, I'm a dark thing unfolding
in a wash of light. I watch the others fall and rise around me.

THE OLDEST SONG
IN THE WORLD

In the 1950s, it was thought to be a Sumerian hymn written on clay tablets thirty-four hundred years ago, likely played on an ancient harp. But in 2008, archaeologists discovered fragments of flutes carved from mammoth bones in a cave in southern Germany called Hohle Fels. These instruments date back almost 43,000 years.

Yet the oldest song in the world lives in what prompts us to carve holes in bone, in what prompts us to hold our lips to the holes. The oldest song lives in what makes us believe that breathing through holes in bone will create music. The oldest song waits for us to sing through the holes in our heart in order to release a music that has been there forever.

I don't know how this happens, but every authentic moment is a note: our first breath, our next breath, our first sense of wonder, our next taste of wind, the sudden experience of light, the rise and fall of love, even the puncture of loss and grief. Each is a note that keeps singing itself. Every day, we inhale the music of life, the way we inhale the sky and everyone else's breath. And when we exhale, what comes through our heart is both mine and yours, everyone's and no one's.

It has always been so. To breathe is to sing. To behold is to sing. To love is to be sung. And to open our heart, especially after pain, is to be sung. In ancient Greece, they would place a harp in the ground on top of a hill and wait for the wind to play its strings. Each of us is such a harp, propped in the open. And life plays us. It's playing us right now. There. Can you hear it? It's such an old song, such a fine song, that its most enduring note rings as this soft silence between us. Listen. Can you feel it?

AT TIMES, THEY DANCE

I'm at a concert on a snowy night, sitting between dear friends, when the mandolin player's chording soothes me into closing my eyes. And there, the inner conversation continues: the gravity of my father dying. My soul shouting through my heart, *You have to keep living!* Death whispering in my mind, *Never forget me.* At times, they fight. At times, they dance. At times, they tug at me. Today I saw an old woman leave crumbs for birds and, across the way, a young man with his head in his hands. Last week I saw the marks of the oxygen mask deepen my father's cheeks. Now the mandolin brings me back. The love between the instrument and its player has opened a depth in which the troubles that weigh me down and the wonders that lift me begin to swirl. Somehow, as he plays, all my concerns about living and dying and the fiery seed they form awaken the simple being within that tries to carry me through the days. I wonder how this settles in others. I open my eyes, close to tears. Something eternal is very near.

Eye of the Crow

I was watching a crow before dawn peck in the dark. It was looking for dropped seed when the coming light edged its crown, revealing its eye as a luminous star. I realized the crow is made to carry this jewel, its muscles and feathers massed around this gem to protect its time on Earth. It's how the living carry what is eternal for a while. How the messy nest of heart is made to incubate the jewel of love. How the tangle of honest speech is made to carry the diamond we call wisdom. How a body is made to carry the gem of Spirit we call soul. But caught in the tangle and mess, it's hard to see the jewel we carry. It often feels like a pit growing in some perishable fruit. Still, something lighted grows in our center, something our life is made to carry. In this, we steward a gift that comes from those we'll never know and which we'll pass to others who will never know us. This is part of its beauty. The gift lives beyond our names for it and uses *us* to keep its presence in the world.

BURNING OFF WHAT'S UNNECESSARY

Why must the gate be narrow?
Because you cannot pass beyond it burdened.

WENDELL BERRY

Joy is the happiness that doesn't depend on what happens.

BROTHER DAVID STEINDL-RAST

We're born with only what's necessary, and as we move in the world, we gather things, the way trees gather moss. In time, we get covered, filmed over by ideas and experiences and memories that mute and scar us. And so, there's a need to return to what we were born with, only wiser. The chief way this happens is beyond our control. As a meteor entering the atmosphere burns off its excess, a life moving through time burns off what's unnecessary. This is a human form of erosion, wearing away what's not essential. Learning and love are the other ways to wear away what's not essential. But being stubborn, we often resist the softer graces, and so need to be eroded back to what matters. No one is exempt from this demanding process. Of course, the burning off is painful. How could it not be? It's a mysterious initiation, and hard as it is to endure, only what will last remains. Like a stone netted in branches held over a fire, we are in time burned free of our entanglements. Who would have imagined such a fate? Who could have imagined the ways life covers us and then sets us free? And yet, on the other side, we are bare and smooth and sturdy, if we can help each other through.

ON THE EDGE
OF GOD'S SHIMMER

Lives unlike mine, you save me.
I would grow so tired were it not for you.

NAOMI SHIHAB NYE

I must confess that cancer ruined me for small talk. I seem drawn only to the core of things. When younger, it came through like fire and scared off others. But with the years, it has thinned into light and others come. I am not alone in this. It's how we learn to love each other. Our fires don't lessen but refine and transform over time into a light we can't resist. I've grown in the light of so many. All of us suns that don't know we're shining.

Especially you. I am in awe of your heart and don't know why God has granted me this special grace to live with you. For what you love comes to life, including me. Your love has turned me inside out, until the moment of loving and being loved bursts open with all its surprises to coat the world with a strange and beautiful honey. I feel it as I write this.

If we live long enough, the fire we carry dies down, and the light we're left with coats our darkness. I feel certain that we knew this in the beginning, but wanting so many things made us forget.

BECOMING CONSCIOUS

I can only speak of my personal journey. I have chanced into wakefulness, more like someone lost coming upon an unimagined vista than through any grind of achievement. Struggling to understand, my mind has been illumined from within, while experience has worn holes in the walls of my ignorance. And worn enough from within and without, the light of all-that-is has flooded me. At first, I rushed to bring loved ones along, but they found me too intense and strange. Then I meant to forego the world and leap, arms open, into the field of unknowing. Only to land here, in the unwavering joy of drifting together through the days. Each time we wake, we become more anonymous. Becoming conscious is shedding what everyone has told you and whispering to the stars what the water coming into spring has learned by being ice.

THIS TENDERNESS

We keep looking for a home though each of us *is* a home. And no matter where we run, we land before each other, thoroughly exposed. This is the purpose of gravity—to wear us down till we realize we are each other. Though we think we're alone, we all meet here. Though we start out trying to climb over each other, we wind up asking to be held. It just takes some of us longer to land here than others. Once worn of our pretense, it's hard to tolerate arrogance. Once humbled, it's hard to withstand a litany of "me." Once burning off the atmosphere of self-interest, there's a tenderness that never goes away. This tenderness is the sonar by which we sense the interior of life. This tenderness is the impulse that frees us. For anything is possible when we let the heart be our skin. The point is to feel whatever comes our way, not conclude it out of its aliveness. The unnerving blessing about being alive is that it can change us forever. I keep discovering that everyone is loveable, magnificent, and flawed.

In Our Rawness

Life expands and contracts in the yoke of a second. One minute there's an unseeable vastness between life and death, and the next, it's the length of a needle we've dropped and can't seem to find. There is no one name or reason or label we can put on what we go through, though all of us, in our want to calm our fears, try to pin it down. Yet when doing all we can—holding, listening, bearing witness, and resisting the demon of "why" while leaning into the angel of "how"—there's so much wisdom in the depths of our rawness. In being so present and engaged, we are forever shaped and carved as we shape and carve. This only makes us a more finely wrought instrument. So you are not blind and thickheaded, no matter how powerless you might feel. Quite the opposite: you are a clear jewel being burnished until all of life is reflected through your deeply exposed heart.

CATCHING FIRE

Those who know the land say there are good fires that let the soil regenerate. It's a hard lesson, but this is true of inner land. To be honest, who I am has burned to the ground more than once. Though it's still too early to tell if these were good fires or not. What keeps us going, thank God, is how we hold each other in place long enough to burn off what's unnecessary and how we save each other when the fire starts to take too much. You could say this is where the Fire of Truth meets the Fire of Love. One day, quite by accident, we set aflame the false selves we've tried on and hold each other to the heat till the illusions we've carried start to burn. In time, if blessed, we simmer into the lake of beauty we all came from. I sensed all this when burning up, the instant you pulled me from the fire of my own making.

THE MANSIONS WE DREAM OF

I have longed for people I thought I would die without. And wanted books and music I was sure would bring me peace. And I've driven myself to accomplish things I thought would secure my worth. And though I seldom touched what I longed for or got what I wanted or achieved what I pushed for, the remnants of my longing burned like ancient wood on the fire of my soul, making the heart of my being burn brighter. To my surprise, I loved and worked and pushed till I used my self up. To my surprise, using my self up was the fate under all my aspirations. At the end of all we want, we're meant to glow. So long and want and dream till you exhaust your heart's desire. We learn so much from longing, and wanting, and dreaming. Mostly, that they are not the mansions we dream of living in, but the wood that keeps our fire going.

THE DILATION OF
WHAT SEEMS ORDINARY

Just now, it happened again. My defenses were down, my memory machine asleep, my dream machine tired, and so the Mystery—which is always beaming in all directions—made it through. And the moment of clarity the Mystery releases is always like a return from amnesia. So this is what it means to be a person, how could I forget: *To be alive, to look out from these small canyons called eyes, to receive light from the sun off the water and feel it shimmer on the water in my heart. To listen to the silence waiting under our stories, long enough that all the vanished words said over time simmer together to make me feel journeys beyond my own. Till I surface before you with a humbled sense of happiness. Not because I'm any closer to what I want, or even know what I want. But because in the flood of all that is living, I am electrified—the way a muscle dreams under the skin that holds it of lifting whatever needs to be lifted.*

BEFORE THE WATERFALL

When lost and confused, I've stood in the cold, on the edge of some storm, suddenly certain of life's unshakeable worth. I don't know how this works. But no matter how we debate if life has meaning, the being inherent in everything receives all our doubt, the way the Earth soaks up rain. It seems we let meaning in by listening to what every simple thing has to offer. For sincerity is the instrument we're born with. And when I'm empty enough to receive you, a fullness is born. When the pain I let out finds the pain you are hiding, love is born. When we can face what is ours to face, and feel what is ours to feel, the heart of our heart shows itself, and we stand before the waterfall of meaning where blessing after blessing pours over our sores till we assume our full stature in the bliss of being ordinary.

SATURN'S RETURN

It takes Saturn twenty-nine years to orbit the sun, to return to where it began. Today is twenty-eight years since the tumor on my brain vanished. And I've returned to the sudden aliveness I fell into after being tossed about and shaken awake. I've tumbled through the years, scoured by life till there's nothing in my pockets, till the folds of my heart are tender and clean. Early on, I clung desperately to the raft of my dreams, bouncing along. Trying to stay upright. Trying to steer away from the rocks and fallen limbs. Trying to get back into the fast part of the current. But since my father died and your mother passed, since we lost our beloved dog Mira, the roar has stopped, and I'm being carried quietly into a greater sea. I feel the swiftness and clearness of life opening before me. Now there's no point in steering, as there's nowhere to go. There's so much more to receive and learn, so much to see through and understand. The rain this afternoon comes from another world. The wet leaves on the bare trees are a resting place for patches of wisdom. I feel like the swan I saw this morning drifting on the lake. I feel complete. Bound to this life, as long as it will have me.

FINDING THE
EXTRAORDINARY
IN THE ORDINARY

When you wake up, everything changes and nothing changes.
If a blind man realizes that he can see, has the world changed?

DAN MILLMAN

I t's a secret hidden in the open, that when fully here, we can find the extraordinary in the ordinary. Beauty is everywhere. What matters is in every small thing. What gives life beams below every surface. It is we who lose track of what matters, because the currents of life are jarring and even battering. Yet the miracle of life is always present. We are the ones who can't stay awake long enough to remember where we last saw it. This is one reason we need each other, to help us refind beauty and truth. This is why the mystic poet William Blake declares that you can "see a world in a grain of sand and Heaven in a wild flower." As all of life is encoded in a trace of DNA, the barest fragment we stumble on holds all of the Mystery, whether it's in the wing of a dragonfly resting on the water or in a bit of glass ground on the curb. This is why the cry of one broken heart reveals the heartache carried throughout history, why the rare instant of peace reveals the well of all peace at the bottom of all souls. The many practices of living prepare us for this refinement of vision, so we can find what matters in what seems mundane.

TALKIN' IT OVER AT OUZOS

Sinatra's voice is piped above us, singing the anthem of our culture, *I did it my way*. We shake our heads. How we're schooled to run from death by playing God, when the deeper journey begins when "My Way" fails. The moments that sustain us are beyond our plans, quietly spectacular. For instance, George was sitting in the sun, watching tennis, and the hot dog was suddenly delicious. The light was dripping from the trees, and the breeze went through the net like time through wounds. The world had opened up. He's still excited, "These moments are why we're here!" I lean forward. He slaps the table, "No need to get high! Just enter your moments!" We stumble quickly into the weight of living. What about all those things to do, to get ahead of? And what about the moments that wait like pearls inside the dive and pry and shell of hard work? And what about greed? Not just for money, but wanting to go everywhere, to experience everything, wanting to be it all. "Wouldn't four moments like this be better than one?" he asks. "They don't add up," I blurt out, "They all lead back to the same moment." We lose track of who's talking. We're in our own moment now. Even Sinatra seems a disembodied angel stuck between worlds because of his insistence on his dream. The aliveness is swirling between us. I know music doesn't end but goes below our hearing into the body.

YOUR PRESENCE

I remember the day I first saw you, really saw you. Your soul flooded from your eyes following a feeling you dared to feel all the way. In that moment, I began to love you. Fifteen years later, your presence and I have many conversations. As you fall asleep, your lids have a sheen. Sometimes, I kiss them and you flutter, feeling it as a wind pushing warm water against you in your dream. We're long past the notion that we can save each other, but we depend on each other. Who I am relaxes in your presence. The way the right amount of light intoxicates a bird to open its wings. These are not alternate realities. I carry aspects of your presence with me. It helps me through the days. As I hold you now, our dog breathes heavily against your legs. I realize, after all this way, you are a bright fish, born to chase any burst of light, to lose yourself in where that burst takes you. It's why animals love you, why they think, *she's one of us.*

UNFILTERED

I drip honey in the bottom of the mug, pour the steaming water, and swirl it with a spoon. I lick the spoon and bring the tea upstairs. The light, climbing over Tom's roof two streets away, streaks through the maple in Lindy's yard and spills through my window, which has no screen. I took it out to let the light in. I've tried to lift the screen from my mind, from my heart, to pry the grid off my past. As I sip my tea, the light spills on the corkboard near my desk where I keep my tribe. The soft light awakens their pinned faces. They seem to breathe. The six who've become brothers along the way. The torn postcard of Pissarro, white beard splattered with paint. The print of Louis Armstrong, his trumpet sweating in his hand. The faded photo of Robert and me, caught twelve springs ago, just ending a hug, surprised we're still here. And near-century-old Joel whose Lithuanian eyes carry the fire. The light starts to move on. It bows its way off my desk, the glow now on Ganesh standing watch. His one hand says come. His other says stay. His huge ears are listening. The light goes on, bringing others into the tribe.

TILTED TOWARD THE SKY

Last night I dreamt of my long history with mirrors. When young, I worked so hard to see myself. First, I polished whatever surfaces I could find. Then I studied my reflection. This was helpful as far as it went. But like all mirrors, everything appeared in reverse, which I forgot at times, and things seemed inverted. In time, my favorite mirror became tarnished, and there was a slight tint to everything. After a while, I stopped using mirrors because I grew tired of only seeing me.

It was then I tossed my mirror in the yard, and it leaned against a tree. The snow melting in March wore a hollow in the ground, and the mirror tilted toward the sky. Now I could see more than myself. For so long I only used half of what reflection can offer.

When the mirror fell even closer to the ground, it revealed the stars. Now I never look into a mirror head-on. And there, behind and around us, all that precedes us and all that awaits us. There, when I least expect it, the spread wings of my better self, waiting.

HOW MANY WAVES

Just as I'm writing a book about listening, I learn that I'm losing my hearing. It goes back to the bloody chemo twenty years ago. It poisoned the cilia in my ears. Now I curse and thank the dark protocol that dripped like syrup in my veins. It made me crawl inside my skin. But here I am: scarred, numb, ulcered, cold. Now everything at the end of conversations is lost and blurred. Now I'm drawn to small things, like what my grandmother said to soothe the stranger suddenly at her door when I was visiting as a child. I want to know how many flaps a gull has to make from sea to cliff. And how many waves it takes to round the edge of a knife thrown in the sand after almost hurting yourself. Where do all the secrets go? In what trunks? In what basements? And what is the story of those who locked them? What do we think we're hiding and from whom? Listening harder doesn't help. Getting closer does.

THE INFINITE CANVAS

We start to talk about death and, of course, that leads to more understanding of life. Just the other day, on the side of a mountain, I saw a tree sway, and it was comforting. It's how I view my time on Earth: just one tree in sway, one brushstroke in the infinite canvas. And yesterday, the peonies, grown to full beauty, couldn't keep their heads up. The weight of their beauty made them bow. As for me, I know I will thin into place like that tree swaying before no one. And you might be that peony forced to bow, not so much to be humbled but because dropping your eyes will let the secret of your beauty show. But tell me, who taught us to record what we see as knowledge, only to confirm it to ourselves as truth? Oh, I want to stay in conversation with you for a very long time. Till our talk undoes the talker, unraveling the mouth of Eternity. Under all our names, we have but one, which waits like an ocean for us to enter. When together like this, in the open, I feel the one name. I find comfort in the vastness and your company.

INSIDE PRACTICE

In another part of the world, small brilliant fish mouth
pebbles along the ocean floor, sucking bits of food, spitting
back the rest. They show us how to suffer and move on. And
high in the Himalayas, away from the eyes of others, a small
cave drips its singular drip as the heartbeat of the mountain.
Here the empty center shows us how to be, one drop of
clearness at a time. When we look closely with our whole
being at anything—at the branches of the human heart or
the silvery glide of fish—the same deep instruction appears.
But it's for each of us to see for ourselves. Try watching dust
lift and settle when you blow on it. Or stare at the paw print
of your neighbor's retriever till it turns into an unexpected
symbol that tells you how to retrieve. Wait for the one shell
you brought back from that beautiful shore three years ago
to reveal itself, at last, showing you how to surface from the
deep. When feeling bereft, watch small deer lift their heads at
the sound of your boots packing fresh snow.

The Golden Thread

The thread on the border of the fabric painting of Mount Fuji—stitched so many years ago, so many oceans away—has held the scene together longer than I've been alive. And on this uneventful morning, the soft rain makes the oak outside my window dip enough for the early light to stream across the braided mountain hanging on my wall. Now the thread on the border swells with the sun and seems for the moment the source of all strength. Then the sun steps higher in the sky, and the thread that holds all things together goes back to work.

Always Building
and Mending

Into God's Temple of Eternity drive a golden nail.

A NOTE LEFT IN THE POCKET OF ARCHITECT RAYMOND MORIYAMA
UPON HIS GRADUATION, BY HIS FATHER WHO LOST EVERYTHING
IN JAPAN DURING WORLD WAR II

We're always building and mending, tinkering and repairing, creating and recreating. It's how the heart uses the mind to affirm that we're here. The way a bird twigs together a nest in spring, we twig together another dream after each disappointment. The way an ant moves the earth, grain by grain, to form its little hill, we move the facts of our life around, grain by grain, to form another home. We do the same with relationships, always building and mending, always coming together and breaking apart. We call this process love. We know the bounce from disappointment to dream as resilience. It's how we thread our suffering through the eye of the needle we call hope, all to stitch and weave something that will keep us warm in the night. Everyone alive participates in this human cycle of build and mend. It's how the Universe keeps growing. While each disappointment feels so large, so destructive, falling and getting up is the exercise by which the muscle of life breaks itself down in order to get stronger. And though the gap between disappointment and repair can seem like a canyon, we work through this synapse repeatedly.

It's what the world asks of us. We're not meant to arrive in some uninterrupted lake of peace. We're meant to flex and grow as the living tissue of a living Universe, while affirming the Whole of Life that we serve.

TRYING TO MAP THE RIVER

That the map you were given doesn't work doesn't mean you were lied to, though this might be. More, that since your grandfather mapped the river, the course of things has changed. Our job is to update the map. Knowing that someday *our* map will no longer fit. Because the life of that river, the story of that river, the maps left by those who lived along the river—none of this stands still. There is only the unexpected moment when the soul, the heart, the world, and the sun are briefly aligned; when what you feel, what I feel, what the world needs, and what life has to offer fills our cup. All we can hope is that the river will round us and quench us with its many tellings.

PILOT LIGHT

As soon as I talk about it, it moves out of view. Let me try again. There is a teacher, a teaching, a moment that keeps working me. I became aware of it four years ago when I met with burn survivors, heroic individuals whose faces have been removed. They have nowhere to hide. Inside is outside for them. Each is a lantern broken by the storm, their flicker steady and bright though everything that covers them is shattered. Two years later, my own struggle to lose weight opened me to those who are covered by too much. I realized no one sets out to be overweight. And since, I've had silent conversations while riding the train, the obese man's eyes shouting: "I don't know how this happened. I'm not what you see! I woke up in this mountain. I'm trying to get out!" The teacher, the teaching, the moment was saying: *You see, some are stripped away, and some are buried. But everyone is in there.* And just last week, my good friend Eileen lost her mother, Margaret, at eighty-eight. At the funeral home, I was fixed on this picture of Margaret when she was thirty-five. Her eyes kept sparking with a sense of self and a sense of what holds up the world. Things I never saw in her Alzheimer's eyes. Now at the grave, I'm watching one of her ancient friends sigh as small birds named Margaret fly from her mouth. Is this the passage no one can escape? Must we all struggle through not being seen for who we are? Is this the turning point in our journey? Is being who we are *anyway* the threshold? We are all burned. We are all buried. We are all trapped in some way by the cataract of years. We are all steady and bright within. So pass nothing or no one by. The light is on. The teacher, the teaching, the moment is waiting.

AROUND THE WORLD

It's been years since I mentioned you by name, but tonight, in the Ark in Ann Arbor, brought by friends to see this young guitar player, I feel you near. This kid is for real. He's got the gift. And nothing excites me more than seeing someone being completely who they are. He drifts into a flow of minor chords that I recognize from late nights when I would lean against the radiator and watch you play in your apartment. It's hard to remember how we hurt each other.

On the way out, I feel all the friendships I've created, broken, and mended. It seems this is our work. I drive us home. In the rear-view mirror, I can see my loved ones sleeping. It's starting to rain, and if I didn't need to see the road, I'd let the wipers rest. It makes me smile and ache at once, to realize it's the utter ease of being who-we-are in front of each other that lets us know we're home.

I love each of you as you sleep. I love the rain rinsing the windshield. I still love my old friend, though I don't know where he is. Whenever we let our love out, something unseen reaches around the world, the way a small wind pushes a patch of water into a wave that after a thousand miles nudges a broken shell ashore, where a child picks it up and holds it to her ear. In this way, our love covers the Earth.

ACCESSING RESILIENCE

For all we go through, for all the heartache and loss, for all the messy ways we're dropped into the depth of life, for all the ways we're pried opened by great love and great suffering, I feel certain there is something unbreakable and regenerative about the force of life we each carry. And while we are the very breakable human container that carries that essence, the Spirit we carry is not. Somehow, resilience comes from letting what's unbreakable rise through the broken pieces that make up our lives. And the only way to access what's unbreakable is through an open heart. And the only way to open our heart is by staying committed to the depth of our feelings. Though we resist their intensity, being rinsed by the depth of our feelings is what opens our heart to its timeless bottom. And following our heart to its timeless bottom is what lets us drink from the unbreakable stuff of life. Whenever I dare to take what I feel to the bottom of my personality, I dip into the well of all personality and I'm renewed.

AFTER THE WAR

To be told by my grandmother of her infant niece thrown against a wall in a cold, dark time. This never goes away. To be brought into another child's life sixty years later. To imagine that she is my grandmother's niece returned. To say nothing to this child when she asks about God. To simply bring her into a field of wildflowers when the sun is high. To whisper, as she runs with delight, *All things are true, though all are not necessary.*

A STAR AFTER RAIN

Does the wave doubt the ocean that lifts it?

Because I'm tired today, my mind opens beyond its net of thought. And I can see that if light can travel for millions of miles, only visible this February afternoon on the bark of a cold oak, why not an ancient cry surfacing across a thousand years of silence? Feeling this, how can anyone doubt the existence of all that can't be seen? Every dancer begins with the steps of ghosted dancers, and every love reaches with the ache of hands now gone. Soon it will be night, and all that carries us will be busy carrying us. In the morning, I will wake like a star after rain, knowing that one self peels away to uncover the next. One dream sheds to disclose the next. One way of thinking flakes off to reveal a beginner's mind. And each attempt to love uncovers our want to be held. Now, watching this cold oak in winter, I realize that in the beginning, everyone told me to ready myself for the hard work of having to get somewhere, though no one knew exactly where we were going. But living has taught me that everything unfolds to reveal a common moment that renews us with its soft and persevering light. So when we're tired enough to reach for each other, when we're stopped by a taste of wonder—like the soft light on the bark of a cold oak—let yourself feel the very stuff of life using our love as a conduit to keep the world going.

NEXT OF KIN

I traveled a long way by plane, then car, then walked past the edge of a forest to a retreat center on Vancouver Island in British Columbia, where I listened to each of them for days. One stilled her shaking hand and said it was in the woods that she first sang, at a patch of light coming through the canopy of trees. Another closed her eyes to conjure her stepdad. He'd slap his hand on the table and say, "It's time for a heart to heart!" He's gone, but she admits how, in a soft moment, he'd lean forward in his wheelchair, lift an imaginary glass, and say, "A toast to the Captain." And the gentle one, who stumbled on her Swiss uncle phoning a friend in Canada at 11:00 to see if they knew what the other was thinking. And the teacher, whose teacher was found as a baby in the garbage. How big her heart was. How she would say to those so quick to judge, "Fucking up is a qualification." And the one who blamed her dead father for everything till she dreamt that the spot of God in her bled into the spot of God in him. I sat among them the way a lost traveler sits in a meadow being washed of his weariness by the creaks and moans of ancient trees and the songs of birds that can't be seen. The truth is we are everywhere: feeling alone, but eager to meet at the well, whenever silence parts our worry.

ALWAYS BUILDING
AND MENDING

I start each day by opening the blinds and making coffee for my wife. This way, I enter the day by letting in light and doing something for someone I love. From there, come what may, I'm centered in the strength of light and care. Then I feed our dog and go to work, which for me is re-entering my conversation with life. Like an astronomer who spends his days looking into the galaxy, tracing the movement of stars and planets, I look into the inner galaxy, tracing and mapping what I can.

By midmorning, I take Zuzu, our yellow Lab, for a walk. It's there that the trees and birds begin to speak. Or rather, I begin to listen, as they've been sharing their secrets constantly. Most mornings, I see birds tending and feeding their young, flying to and fro with twigs, or pecking at the ground for seed. They're always building and mending their makeshift nests. Much like us, going to and fro to gas up the car, and pay the bills, and get the tools we need to patch the roof. Endless tasks that keep us a part of life.

Today, we went for our walk a little closer to noon. The sun was everywhere and things seemed extra close. Perhaps my mind was more empty and my heart more full, but the tulips just opening and the wind ruffling the budding leaves seemed Eden-like. Then I saw a single bird perched atop the very tip of an enormous blue spruce. So easily balanced, it looked out on the world it would have to return to. Then I saw another perched atop an old oak.

The birds pausing from their tasks became silent teachers, saying without saying that we need to fall in love with the ordinary rhythms of life, again and again. And when the tasks are done or have become too heavy to complete, we need to pause and perch atop our worries and concerns. So we can return to the world and do what needs to be done, until what sustains us reveals itself like the inside of a seed cracked by our beak.

I start each day by letting in light and doing something for someone I love, in order to do what needs to be done to repair our small part of the world. Then I listen, and that listening becomes the perch from which I chance to see all we are a part of. The day unfolds and I get excited, then annoyed, then confused, and tired. I eat and sleep and do it all over again. When I get tangled in the tasks, it can seem like hell. But when the light illuminates the inside of things, like today, and the coffee is brewed, things go quiet, and there's nothing else I could ask for.

THE STRENGTH
OF OUR ATTENTION

I have a mind to confuse things,
unite them, bring them to birth,
mix them up, undress them,
until the light of the world
has the oneness of the ocean.

PABLO NERUDA

Our heads are round so our thoughts can change direction.

FRANCIS PISSARRO PICABIA

Whenever we feel burdened and lost, or fragmented and bereft, the strength of our attention is a way back to feeling vital and alive. What this means is that as water will fill any hole, life-force will fill us and animate us, if we can release our full attention. It doesn't matter to what, just that we try one more time to be completely present and hold nothing back. The oldest tools of presence are holding and listening. These are the instruments of attention that never seem to fail. When we can attend whatever is before us, we become immersed. And no one can be immersed without being brought alive. There you have it. As far away as care might seem, we only have to cross the barrier of our weariness to begin again. Still, it can seem impossible when weighed down. That's when we need the attention of others, to be curious when we're numb, to bring us water when we think we can't drink, and to feed us wonder when we think there's none left in the world. As a cut will heal, the strength of our attention will mend a cut in our outlook, if we give ourselves again to life.

WITH THINGS THAT BREAK

What matters bears entering more than once. This entering-more-than-once is a form of listening. It's how leaves in fall offer a deeper color on rainy days. In that grayness, we look again, and the undertones have a chance. I have a friend who moved to Victoria, that lush island city off the coast of Vancouver where winters are long and dreary. In her third winter, someone born there pulled her aside and said, "You have to learn to love the rain. You have to spend more time wet. Then you'll have different names for lazy squall and slanting mist. Then the rain, as much as the sun, will cause something in you to grow." It's the same with things that break our heart. Like learning to love the stories of elders who repeat themselves. You have to learn to love the slant of their rain. To take the time to sense what they can't leave behind. With things that are new, we keep moving. With things that break, we circle back, repeating and renaming till we find each other in the rain.

SWAYED IN ALL DIRECTIONS

I doze in the hammock, and this book of voices from long ago falls from my lap into the grass. And these ancient voices say to me in my sleep, *While you are not suffering, give to those who are*. When I wake, the page where Li Po spoke of dead soldiers' horses wailing to the sky is stained by the grass. The wind lifts my face to the east where we are at war in our own time. How do I hold the suffering of others in the middle of such a calm and beautiful day? We each can do the breaking. We each can be broken. We each can hold. We each can be held. I feel powerless in the presence of such suffering, and yet it's the strength of our attention that makes a difference. The breath of this day keeps lifting my head. Is it enough to be kind where we are?

BETWEEN TROUBLES

The old painter tells me that he loves to drive through small towns, so he can sketch the light and strike up conversations with the young woman who pumps his gas and the lobster fisherman who lets him bait his traps. He loves to meet life as it bubbles up between troubles. Last summer, he wanted to meet that poet from Nebraska, the one who speaks so simply of all that matters. He didn't want to bother him, just to say how grateful he is for what his poems open. Eight hundred miles later, he was asking for the poet in the old bookstore. Then he drifted into the antique store in Garland where he bought four lanterns. It's there the owner said, "Oh Ted, he lives in Dwight." So the painter took his lanterns and drove the back road to Dwight where he left a note on Ted's window that read, "Your poems matter." Once home, he set up the lanterns and confessed that he needs more light as he talks to death. The next day, he painted a barn he saw in Dwight and sent it to Ted. In telling me this, he's all aglow, a lantern himself. He takes my hand and wells up, "I love this life."

THE WAY WE PRACTICE

The Earth spins on its axis drifting through the dark, seeming to go nowhere as it inches its way around the sun. What if this is the way of things? What if every heart spins on its story? What if every mind spins on its best guess of how this all goes together? What if the very cells—in stone, bird, fish, and camel—spin on their little nodes of life-force inching their hosts to heal and grow? What if our particular lives spin on the axis we call spirit, each of us inching our way through the dark around God? What if love is the way we practice spinning about each other until the holiness of things appears?

As I'm spinning, you come running. Seeing the light on your face stops my endless thinking. You take me to the bluebird house where six of the smallest birds I've ever seen are quivering—their seedlike beaks gaping for food. Just below all thought, everything is aquiver and true.

VELLUM

Up early, I'm softened by the light in Rich's library when I find this manuscript page framed and hanging in a corner. It rests on a wall in a home thousands of miles and hundreds of years from where it was created. Amazing that anything so delicate could last. It is only three by seven inches. A leaf from a Latin Bible copied by hand in Bologna in the thirteenth century. Now it hangs in the corner of a book lover's home in Indianapolis.

There's something about this leaf that holds everything. Not that it's from a Bible. More that some inner knowing crept across someone's mind centuries ago stirring them to write it down. And someone else hundreds of years later was asked or paid to copy it, slowly and beautifully. Then somehow, the leaf escaped decay and fire and neglect and the rightful dissolution of forms. Through curiosity or chance, it was tucked in the bottom of a trunk that was placed in the bottom of a steamer that crossed the ocean. Now it's outlived those who knew anything about it.

I can feel their efforts. To be suddenly stirred by something unseen. Then taking turns, as we try to preserve the efforts of others. Passing it with care from stranger to stranger. Until when passing what matters, we don't feel so strange.

I can't stop thinking of the illiterate scribes who didn't understand what they were copying. They only felt the softness of the vellum they lettered on, the thin, lasting paper made from the skin of unborn or stillborn animals. I close my eyes and wonder if these scribes were enlivened more from touching the skin of the unborn than from the strange words they copied. Is this the lesson beneath the words? Are the words just an excuse? A reason to carry the skin of all that is yet to be born?

I'm compelled by the vellum of our consciousness, the softness of our stillborn hearts waiting to come alive. Rich is up. He finds me as one who's tripped over a treasure. He takes the frame from the wall and the leaf from its frame and we touch it together.

THE CREATIVE STORM

We drive an hour north to Meijer Gardens, a sweet amphitheatre carved into a small hill. As we file in with our coolers and lawn chairs, the summer stage and soft clouds drifting behind the shed make it seem like a hill outside of Athens twenty-five hundred years ago. We've come to hear Chick Corea and Béla Fleck, two jazz legends drawn together by their love of the unknown.

As they begin, their virtuosity is obvious. Relaxed and focused, they seem to be doing nothing while doing everything. I can feel the long devotion necessary to trip so easily into wonder. Imagine climbing stairs made of water to a doorway of light, through which we both leave ourselves and find ourselves. This is the rush of unity that musicians and artists and lovers know when they give themselves completely to their music and their art and to what they love.

Look—the pianist's fingers float faster than any mind can direct, and the graying banjo player spans octaves with the ease of a heart trusting all that it hears. The clouds part as the two improvise, chasing each other like goldfinch in the sun. And the creative storm circles us. Instead of debris, this storm leaves *The Köln Concert* by Keith Jarrett, and "Ode to Joy" by Beethoven, and "Jupiter" by Mozart. And here in a piece Chick and Béla call "The Enchantment," it appears again, as eighty years of playing obeys the flutter of notes running through their hands.

Tonight, the creative storm is strong, rising as the sun goes down. It's here. Look—a gust of wind swirls their sheet music across the stage. The pianist and the banjo player close their eyes and just keep going, through years of calluses and broken strings. Look—the instruments are playing themselves, like two fast brooks headed for the sea.

169

AS THE SNOW FALLS

There is much to say about him. But it's best to stay immediate. He is ninety-nine, born a world away, a painter who during the day is in conversation with light. Once, when he was eighty-nine, after a long afternoon together, he surfaced at the end of a path we walked in silence and said, "I'm tired of words. Words, words, words. I want to listen to the light."

Today I drove four hundred miles to ask him, "After a century, what do you see? What does the light say?" He paused and stared off, then told me that he has the same dark dream about the Holocaust. Can't stop seeing his frightened relatives shot in a trench in Lithuania. He wants to paint panels in which the trees bear witness. With the sweep of charcoal, he wants to show how trees lament, as if his whole life has led to this.

He takes my arm with the strength of someone much younger and tells me that, in the dream, it is strangely quiet, that as the snow falls, the lost souls rise. This is the image that won't let me be: as the snow falls, the lost souls rise. Perhaps the snow agrees to take their place on earth, so the mistreated can come to rest in the sky.

There are long silences between his words, not because he's forgetful, but because he remembers and hears so much. I think the older we get, the deeper we dive for what to say.

He and I swim in and out of silence all afternoon, like old dolphins. I love to watch him stare off, as if his deep attention is keeping the unseen angels and demons from destroying each other.

It's hard to say goodbye. He walks me to the car, hugs me firmly, and whispers, "Be strong." I kiss his cheek. He says, "You have a gift. Trust it, hone it, protect it."

I watch him in the rearview mirror waving his cane as I drive away.

In Full Praise

When asked about the difference between a slow-witted boy and a sage, a rabbi said, "No difference. They both depend on humility and praise." His students were puzzled. He went on, "When unaware, we grow like a stone. When awakened, we break through like a sapling." They still seemed confused. He continued, "When self-conscious, we dart like a rabbit, never in the open for long. We watch for others and watch ourselves chew." He went further, "But when embodied, we live like a tortoise rising from the deep, in full praise of the bottom, humble to surface in the world." Some were nodding, while others scrunched their brows. He sat down among them, "Each of us is beautiful and worthy, no one more holy than another. And each of us is part stone, part sapling, part rabbit, part tortoise." His students were busy identifying with one or the other when a small boy dropped his head, unable to find himself anywhere. This opened the rabbi even more, "Don't despair. For trees grow out of stone. And rabbits will chew on their leaves. And love itself will awaken the tortoise hiding on the bottom."

THE UNHEARD SYMPHONY

What if it's neither you who touch nor me who is touched? What if the moment of touch lets us join in a current of aliveness that is always there? What if our love lets us see what we stand on in the middle of a dark time, the way lightning lets us see the earth at night? What if there is only one chord heard many ways? What if I've spent all these years trying to learn new chords, when I sorely need to absorb the one? What if all depends on our presence and attention? What if this is all we ever have? Could this be the secret of love: that it grows our presence like a seed, causing us to reach for each other till our reach itself bears fruit? What if birds are notes longing for a clarinet and fish are tones yearning for a violin, and the flow of life below our names is a calligraphy that sweeps us into gestures we call our lives? What if the unheard symphony writes itself? When I hush my mind, I feel like snow the instant it is closer to the ground than the sky.

Letting Everything
In and Through

Let me keep surrendering myself
until I am utterly transparent.

PSALM 19

The ultimate value of staying open is that we're scoured clean of all that might burden us: memories, wounds, assumptions, and conclusions—even the debris of unworkable dreams. And more important than what we reach for or aspire to is the cleansing release of all that takes up residence in the reservoir of our perception and feeling. For unprocessed experience and unlived dreams clog our arteries of being, and this can be life threatening. So, like it or not, we're asked to let everything in and through, trusting that it's the passage of life through us that is renewing, not what we accumulate or accomplish along the way. As blood must pass through organs, as rivers must empty into the sea, thoughts and feelings must pass through our being, if we're to stay fresh and changeable. After all these years, I've come to see that the aim is not to be empty or full, but to stay an open channel for everything life has to offer. I'm still learning how to do this.

Instructions to
My Smaller Self

When hurt, it's important to scream. Just don't pray to the
scream. When sad, it's important to grieve. Just don't build
a kingdom of your loss. When falling through whatever you
thought would last, admit, "I'm lost and confused." Just don't
map the world as lost and confused. And when riding the wave,
however it appears, feel the strength in you released. Just don't
believe the strength comes from you alone. But most of all,
when listening to others, say, "This may be so." Then look for
yourself at what life is painting with all its colors.

TIME IS A ROSE

What is time but God undressing Himself of His Mystery hour by hour? Or if it suits you, think of time as the wind of existence moving the pollen of being from one decade to the next. Or as an eternal flute that perpetuates the one song we all try to sing until a child is born with more depth and heart than any one child should have. You can understand time as the unfolding of nature or the workings of physics. Whatever language works for you, any will do. But under all our efforts to name what is unnameable, we're swept along like minnows tucked in the ocean. And while love and suffering let us glimpse the totality of life, it is gratitude that lets us *feel* our place in the Infinite Sway of Things. This is why the life of feeling matters. Because, just as a whale feels the entire surface of the ocean as it breaches, someone moved to help another feels the entire surface of humanity as their care breaches the ocean of circumstance. As a cocoon tears, as bark peels, as the hard casing that grows fruit splits—the casing of our pretense and stubbornness breaks open, so the soul can unfold like a rose and fill the world. This is a fate to be longed for, even though we fear it.

THE CONFLICT
FROM ASSIGNMENTS

The professional photographer takes assignments from "without" . . .
the creative photographer takes assignments from "within" . . .
the conflict from assignments—from "without" versus those
from "within"—often perplexes the serious photographer.

ANSEL ADAMS

Wayne calls from Australia, where he's living with Kelly, south of Sydney, where the South Pacific funnels toward New Zealand. They've found each other and slipped into the eye of the moment. His aperture is wide. I can hear it in his voice. Before Wayne left Santa Fe, our mutual friend, Richie, insisted that he buy the widest angle lens he could. There wasn't a lot of time, but he did. They're both photographers, Richie and Wayne. Now Wayne is telling me about depth of field. You see, the widest lens lets everything in. It filters out nothing, though it's impossible to keep anything but what's right before you in focus. While he was explaining this to Kelly, she brought him into focus and said, "It's you. It's how you take in the world. You can't help it." Now he's on the phone across the seas saying, "And I thought of you. It's what makes you a poet. I know you can't help it." And I thought of Susan and Robert and Richie. It's what makes all of us poets before we step into the world. And none of us can help it.

Letting everything in is a precarious gift that keeps us close to what matters. Think of those you admire who can fall completely into any moment, who so love the smell of garlic that they lead you down that alley to the little Italian place you never knew was there. Think of how that evening is now part of your mythology. We so want to fall this completely into life. Yet not being able to keep anything but what's in front of you in focus is a problem.

There's more. We're on the phone, and Wayne keeps talking. I've always followed his talk. I've known him long enough to understand that he's just trying to cough up the ineffable glitter he feels in the back of his throat. It's where all the things that matter, that we can't keep in focus, go. Wayne is talking now about how great photographers like Ansel Adams extended the exposure of wide lenses. It seems someone along the way discovered, probably by accident, that if you take your time, take a very long exposure, even up to two minutes, then everything—from the lash on your love's eyelid to the snow on the mountains six miles behind her—everything comes into focus. Everything becomes clear.

Ansel Adams was born in his parents' bed. So his intimate focus began right away. When he was four, he was tossed face-first into a garden wall breaking his nose during an aftershock from the 1906 San Francisco earthquake. One of his earliest memories was holding his nose and watching the fire devour much of the city. Now his wide-angle lens was set for life. No wonder he had the patience to let everything in and to be still enough, long enough, for the fires to die down. No wonder he had the resolve to wait for things to become clear.

Now I'm up, as I am every day, just before dawn, and I realize this is what I've learned over the years, what I am devoted to: letting everything in and waiting for the fires to die down, waiting for the light to mix it all together; waiting with a quiet resolve for everything to come into focus. The first part of being an artist or lover is to let everything in. But sooner or later, we're refined by time to let light do its work on the exposure of our heart.

THE GREAT TEACHER

At first, we see ourselves in everything. But experience, the great teacher that it is, inverts this, the way erosion exposes the heart of a mountain. And in slow, irrevocable time, which can't be rushed, we find that everything lives *in us*, the way all of life is encoded in our genes. In just this way, every form of life is imprinted in the heart, revealed when we dare or are forced to feel. For it's through the life of feeling that we come upon the ten thousand teachers, each bringing us more fully alive. So the leaf about to fall from the top of the tree is teaching me how to let go of the one belief that no longer works. And the turtle inching its way across the mud is teaching me how to stay true for the long haul. And you, reaching for me in your kindness, you are teaching me that care is the soft hand of God feeding us, the way an old gardener stops to feed a baby bird.

THE ONE CRY

She was coming of age. The eyes beneath her eyes were beginning to see. It frightened her to meet what we have done to each other: genocide after genocide, all the charred bones fuming with the stories of those they walked in. Taking in the brutality of life was blocking her from all the beauty and wonder. It was at this time that we met. She was being scoured of her innocence. But innocence is only the glare of wonder. It's not wonder itself. Wonder is how beauty still shines in the rain-soaked field after the bodies are buried. She was frightened, not sure if she wanted to be here any longer. I listened till there was no more to say. Just then an ant was carrying a crumb twice its size across the sidewalk. I didn't mention it.

I thought, *She is right to fear the brutality, but the wonder always outlasts the violence, even if we are brought to an end. There is nothing to do but live and meet it all.* After a long while, I said softly, "I no longer ask why, only how." She searched my face to see on what I based my sense of the world. I said, "We push each other to one side or the other, as if dark or light by itself will show us the way."

Just then the ant dropped its crumb and scampered off, but another picked it up and carried on. I looked at my aging hands and confessed, "Somehow, I'm stronger when I'm soft, safer when I let in the paradox of it all." I think she understood. I admitted, "I've stopped trying to turn truth into something else." She finally spoke, "Will I ever get rid of this fear?" I dropped my shoulders, "I don't know. But if fear gathers like a cloud, the majesty of life is always somewhere shining."

HOWEVER IT MIGHT APPEAR

Finally, there is joy in being winded in the open. This might be one antidote to suffering. To let life, however it might appear, move through us cleanly. The way sitting with you when we're too tired to prop up our masks lets us admit what a difficult honor being here really is. Though sometimes we're afraid to hold, all of us want to be held. It makes me reach for someone who has fallen. And when I fall, I hope someone will reach for me. The one cloud hovers around the peak because it knows how lonely things that stand up forever can be.

TO BE RECEIVED

Stan and I met by chance in a café. I was writing and he was playing his music too loud, even through his earbuds. I went to ask him to turn it down when I recognized the song he was listening to. It was Van Morrison's "The Healing Game." We talked for a bit and I went back to work. I'd see Stan in the café a few times a week. We'd say hello, talk for a minute or two, and go to our interiors. He seemed nice, but guarded.

One day in February, I saw Stan jump up and run outside, deftly sliding around his table and others, not spilling a single coffee. A woman had slipped on the ice in front of the café, and Stan was the first to see it happen. He helped her up and guided her inside to an empty table. She was rather shaken. I went over to them and asked the woman, "Are you all right?" She nodded at both of us. I said, "What would you like? I'm happy to get it." She wanted the fuss to be over but dropped her shoulders and said, "Just some tea." I looked to Stan, "You deserve something for sure." He tilted his head and said, "Thanks, a double espresso."

I brought them their drinks and sat with Stan at his little table before he could put his earbuds back in. I asked, "Where'd you learn to move like that?" He smiled but didn't say a word. I sensed he didn't want to talk, and I didn't want to pry. As I was about to leave, he softly said, "I was a medic in Iraq." I sat back down and said, "I can't imagine." He shrugged, "You're right. You can't."

Just then, Hannah, who manages the café, lifted the blinds, and a small arc of winter sun fell on Stan's face. Things lined up, and I could briefly see my way into Stan, like when you stand at the head of a staircase and can see down into a room on the next floor. As guarded as he was, I think he wanted someone to see through him. Watching the woman fall and jumping up to help her got his heart pumping, and he had nowhere to go with it. And since the light got in that far, he seemed to turn so I could get a better view. As if to say, "As long we're here, go on, take a look."

I wasn't sure what was happening. We chatted on the surface for a while, and I looked into Stan, a kind and quiet stranger. While chatting, a deeper part of me went down his stairs to the slightly opened door on the next floor. I opened it slowly. There was a kitchen with a beautiful young woman at the stove. She was upset. A little boy was in a high chair, and Stan was at the table with his head in his heads. I realized at once that the beautiful young woman was on the verge of leaving Stan and taking their boy with her. While there were reasons, it was the fact that he never let her into any of his inner rooms—that was what she couldn't bear.

Was I imagining all this or were we communicating on a mystical level? Stan sipped his espresso and said, "Life just keeps throwing us curves, doesn't it?" I smiled, "For sure. That's why I like the blues." He laughed, and I sensed he was inviting me to look further. I went down his inner hall and was drawn to a dark and heavy door. I opened it and entered the war in Iraq. Gunfire was everywhere, and Stan was tending a soldier whose left leg was blown off. He did what he could, then stroked the poor man's head, muttering, "Just close your eyes and think of home, buddy. We'll get you out of here." Chaos and fear were everywhere. Blood was all over Stan's hands and shirt. He and another medic lifted the legless warrior into a Jeep. They closed the door and tapped the window. The Jeep sped off.

I could tell that Stan returned to these rooms over and over. I wondered if he was entering my inner rooms at the same time. I felt softly privileged that this unexpected intimacy was opening between us, all below words. I thought I'd seen enough, and it felt respectful to leave his rooms as I had found them. I started to go back to my table when Stan said, "Now let me buy you one."

So we continued. There was something else that Stan wanted me to see. As we chatted on the surface, I went down another flight of stairs to what seemed like the basement. There were two large, musty doors. Each had a lock. But when I approached the first, the lock opened itself. This was when I was certain that Stan wanted me to be there.

As I opened the first door, Stan was sixteen, walking home from school to find an ambulance in the driveway. He ran inside to find his father had died of a heart attack. His whole world had shattered. His heart had shattered. His trust in life had broken into sharp pieces of glass. He found his mother sobbing in the living room. His father was in a heap in his chair. Life was exploding. Strangely, the hell of that moment helped him get through the hell of Iraq.

I wanted to go to young Stan and comfort him, but I was an invisible guest. I backed out of that room and shuffled to the final door. As I neared it, its lock opened too. This door opened itself. This was a safe and beautiful time in Stan's life. He was ten or eleven, coming home from school, and his father was greeting him in the driveway, so happy to see him. Every day, his father would swoop him up in his arms, kiss his cheek and ask, "So what did you learn today?"

By now, Stan and I knew each other very well, without speaking about any of it. I could only imagine what he'd seen in me. I said, "That was very kind of you, the way you helped that woman." He shrugged and lifted his espresso, "Thanks for the drink." I smiled, "You too."

I went back to my table, unsure if any of what I'd seen in Stan was true. He put his earbuds back in, and we returned to our interiors. I watched him for a while, certain that we all have an inner house full of winding stairs and hidden rooms. While we may have our reasons, not letting others into our inner rooms makes life unbearable. How resilient we are depends on whether we keep the doors to those rooms open or not. And we never know how much others suffer until they let us in, and we softly enter.

Stan taught me that day that there are a thousand ways to let each other in. So when we meet and I seem too far away, receive me with a coffee and a question. And I'll receive you. If we dare, we can open the rooms in each other's basements and soften the impact of kitchens and wars and sudden deaths before asking, "What did you learn today?"

EVERY CHANCE WE GET

When you've lost something dear, and you can't stop hurting, and everyone around you is full of light, let the lightness they carry soothe your sore heart. Even though you don't want to be touched in your grief. And when everyone around you is hurt, or lost in their grief, or near death, just as you've landed in a small patch of joy, don't feel guilty. Just touch whatever they might touch, without judgment, leaving a trail of softness and acceptance. In time, our grief and our softness find each other, the way light fills every crack. We must not resist either, but open before each other, and fill each other every chance we get.

RECEIVER-OF-THE-WATERFALL

Like a waterfall that shapes its mouth with the force of all that water, the Source has little regard for what it does to us. It simply wants to be expressed in the world. The creative force flows over everyone. Imagine the many waterfalls and rapids that cross the Earth, coursing all at once, each making its song. In just this way, the creative force courses through the souls of the world.

Inherently, each of us is mirrored at birth to some aspect of nature. Some are born to bear the flow and record its song. Some are called to be like earth and hold the roots of all that grows. Still others are born to be like stone and hold things up, while some are meant to be what burns, providing light. We can't choose the element we're born to. We can only grow what we are and learn how to live with it.

I am a *receiver-of-the-waterfall*. This could be a Native American name for a poet. And I would ask for no other fate. I love being worn by the water of life. My angst has been to make sense of what passes through. Yet as I age, as I'm worn more completely, I'm losing the need to arrive at conclusions. More and more, the poems, the art, the metaphors, the ahas are all in the gurgle and flash of any given moment.

LANDING FACE UP

I'm watching the sun rise over the Rockies. The foothills are rounded and closer to the living, as if bowing to let us wander among them, the way a camel might kneel so someone can mount it. Watching the hills so quietly outlive us makes me know how blessed I am to land after sixty-six years into the bones of who I am. Imagine a jagged stone kicked from a ledge by an elk, and as it falls, its edges are broken off and somehow it lands face up. That's how I feel. Lucky to have landed face up with all my edges broken. And living in the open, I'm waiting for the sun one more time. I was in such a fierce hurry when I was young. I had a desperate longing that I couldn't name, which has been broken from me like a tusk caught in a fence. And it's from that break that the river of questions flowed, from which I have been drinking ever since.

How We Make
Our Way

There are only two mistakes one can make along the road to truth:
not going all the way, and not starting.

BUDDHA

It was falling into a moment of jazz that led me to this book. And so, I have to say that I keep making my way by following aliveness wherever I find it, wherever it finds me. Because in moments of aliveness, I see more and take more in. Because when touched by life, either softly or harshly, I feel my place in the larger order of things, the way a knot tugged in one corner of a net pulls at the entire net. When feeling the smallest part of life pull me, I feel the whole net of life tug and sway. This is the sensation of Oneness. And feeling enough of these tugs in the depth of my being, I'm convinced that no other dream is as vital or as life sustaining as the unscripted moment of aliveness. I feel it when I watch my wife sleep, or when I'm thoroughly lost in piano music, or when I'm humbled by the power of the sea. I now think that dreams, of the sort that we imagine and work toward, are just smaller lights that lead us back to this threshold of aliveness. For life only wants to be alive, the way fire only wants to burn. And so we wake, and find each other, and love. There could be no finer destiny.

INSIDE EVERY BURDEN

I don't know why, but for all I've been through—almost dying, almost living, seeking love till I've become love, seeking truth till I've become a question—for all of it, I'm certain that inside every nut is a seed. Inside every fear, a pin of light. Inside every desperation, a drop of being. Inside every loss, an inch of what can never be lost. And inside every burden, a pearl of worth. I don't know why, but I'm certain that the pearl of worth is waiting for us to dive to the bottom of all trouble, to pry the shell of burden open, and to bring the gem we were born to carry to the surface.

CALLING IT IN

Months back, I was feeling sad, not tragic, just depressed enough to feel distorted. I went to Son's for a beer and a game of pool. In the corner, a woman slouching, close to forty-five. A stranger started teasing her. I interceded, which is unusual for me, and went back to my stool. The bartender said, "She's Always Bored. And Boring." She looked raw. He said, "Last week, she called the radio and said her collie was missing. They broadcast it for three days." He was talking too loud for me, "She ain't got a collie. She made it up." I asked if she lived with anyone. He said, "Nah, with that loon?"

What makes me admire her calling it in? Tell me you haven't looked at the phone some days imagining reasons to call. Tell me, please, how she is any different than the drill press operator I once saw drilling little darknesses into metal: head bowed, his arm sinking methodically, bounding back, the whine of metal slivers piling at his feet? And how is his daydreaming while drilling any different than Father Gregory sinking the wafer into countless mouths, repeating with utter sincerity, "Body of Christ . . . Body of Christ . . . Body of Christ."

I repeat things till my sense of what is holy opens, and then I want to call you up, to call it in. I want that space where everything seems to connect: the drill, the press, the countless mouths, the wife of emptiness calling for her collie.

INHERITING NOW

You ask, "How much can one heart hold?" as I lift a rock worn by the stream to its beauty by holding onto nothing. For all the ways we resist, each soul, by the weight of its fundamental being, brings us to the bottom of things where we are worn smooth. I think this abrasion of life-force is a form of inner erosion that every person experiences on Earth. Finally, it's letting go that lets us rest on the bottom. You ask, and all I can say is that teachers wait in the center of every moment to show us that though there are many places to go, they all lead to the same ground of being we all share. In this way, we run through the world, only to be worn to a common center in which we recognize each other at last.

LET THEM GO
WHERE THEY WILL

Last night we saw Eugene O'Neill's *Long Day's Journey into Night* and were let out on Forty-Third Street, unsure of where we stood, throbbing in the rawness of how we all need each other and blame each other for the things we can't explain. The crowds were bumping us along, and I thought that any dream or wound is bright enough or dark enough to trap us. If the one thing we do well becomes where we hide. If our one terrible pain becomes a ditch we can't climb out of. If we can't help each other suffer the weight of what we break.

And so, it's crucial that our feelings be shaken like birds from the tree of our heart. Let them go where they will. Otherwise, we can be trapped in our own story. You will sense the tangle as it starts to happen. Your readiness to position yourself as the hero or the victim will interrupt the moment about to be lived, and you will go on with your drama anyway. That's when we have to drop all narratives like leaves before winter and simply listen—for nothing, to nothing. To listen the way a jellyfish listens to the silent blue with its transparent hood. This chance to drop all excuses has saved me more than once.

It's close to midnight, and I can't yet re-enter the stream of life swarming about us. This being human is a dance that parts the veil between the truth and what we want. Trying when we can to scour our history of perception before it clouds us into thinking that we know where this is going.

THE DEEPEST PLACE ON EARTH

Birgit is from Israel. She doesn't have long to live. We meet briefly in Utrecht outside of Amsterdam. Her sister wheels her into the corner of a small café where I am waiting. Her spirit is glowing, all the more because her body is leaving.

She wants me to know that some deep part of her wants to live, though an equally deep part of her is ready to be done with this. I take her hand and say nothing. I can tell that her heart is flapping like a flag in the Mystery. It's all we can hope for.

She gives me a drawing of a dragon and a stone from the Dead Sea. She says, "It's from the deepest place on Earth." It has seen the fire in the center. As has Birgit. I ask, and she says she's in a lot of pain, except for the moments that she's feeling love. It works this way for all of us.

The three of us fall silent in a fullness beyond words. She goes to thank me when I stop her. She came for something but gave me everything by meeting so softly on the cliff between beauty and suffering, where nothing and everything sing to us in whispers.

LIFE AFTER THE OCEAN

And what of an afterlife? In our humanness, the question stays too small. Like crabs on the bottom asking each other if there is life after the ocean. What if one thing is supposed to carry another? What if the purpose of the snake is to keep the process of shedding alive? And the purpose of being human is to keep the process of loving alive? What if Heaven for the wave is evaporating into sand? And destiny for the fox is that when he dies he will live inside the coyotes that eat him? What if paradise for rain is the root it swells in the dark? What if reincarnation is not one to one, but more like leaves broken down to mulch? What if we disperse into all that we love? What if your kindness becomes part of the lake that held you? And my heart becomes part of the wood that braces a bridge that saved me? And Susan's ability to listen becomes part of the canopy that shades those tired on the way? What if Robert's unshakeable belief in all that is unnamable becomes the bent nail that keeps the barn from falling? What if our tears and sweat irrigate the dreams of those yet to be born?

HOW WE MAKE OUR WAY

When he hits the conga with his palm, it feels like color splashing in a wave. When she bounces the bow lightly on the strings, it feels like stones dropping in a lake. When their offerings circle the old man in the audience, it reminds him of the small hall in Europe where he first heard music as a boy. He can still smell the cigars in the lobby at intermission. The concert ends, and the conga and viola go back to sleep. But he stays longer than the others, feeling at home in the empty hall.

Later, in the outskirts of the city, a thief tired of running stops to pant and hide behind a stone wall built by someone he'll never know. He slouches and looks at the small thing he stole, unsure why he took it. The policeman who will find him has just run a light. He senses he's close but is stopped by a young woman coming out of a club. The moonlight illuminates the tattoo on her ankle. She reminds him of his daughter whom he hasn't seen in two years. The tattoo is of a small bird about to fly. In the soft night, it seems like the part of her he's lost. Now he feels like he's chasing himself.

At the same time, halfway round the world, an old woman fills her pot from the ancient river as her granddaughter watches. The sun coats the lip of the pot, and they carry the water between them back to their small home. The old woman feels the weight of the water moving in the pot and the strain of the little girl. This is how we make our way, carrying the weight between us. A thousand miles away, a farmer's horse stops, and the farmer, who whipped the horse when both were young, undoes the reins and puts his head close to the horse's face, and the same light that coats the lip of the old woman's pot warms their heads.

FOR INSTANCE

I started writing because life took my breath away. It was how when stunned by beauty I tried to stay stunned, how when touched I tried to keep the touch alive. The miracle of sun on water, for instance, when dwelled upon, begins to say, *You see, this is what love can do to pain.* The old woman sifting dried leaves through a large wood-framed screen, who learned this from her mother, is sifting tea in the soft morning wind without a word. Her very presence begins to say, *You see, this is how a broken heart sifts what is true, so it can be steamed into something warm that heals.*

When I put my glasses down and take my hearing aid off, my vision blurs and my hearing falls into a wash, and I lose the distinction between people and nature, between cityscapes and landscapes, between silence and music. In a startling return to miracle, they are at heart all one, as they have always been.

The other day George and I cut up an old cherry tree and sawed a log in half. It was filled with ants who'd been feasting on the knot. They scurried into the grass. Hollowed out, the log was empty. It was then we noticed a line of inner grain that looked like a feather, as if some ancient bird had been turned to wood long before we were born. This is our fate on Earth: to be stunned, to be touched, to eat our way through our knots, till we are light as a feather.

BECOMING A SMALL GESTURE

Maybe all my sufferings have been carving me into a statue of Ganesh that someone will find in the next life in a small store in New York, when they rush in to get out of the rain. Maybe all I've been through will draw them to pick me up and touch my long trunk or one of my four, giving hands. And though they can't afford to take me home, they might circle the store three times before putting me on their credit card. Because something in the way life has carved my eyes shut speaks to the unawakened song they carry, that they so desperately want to sing. Maybe they'll take me home and place me on their nightstand where I can bless them as they dream of being who they are.

In Love with the World

There is no end to love. We may tear ourselves away, or fall off the cliff we thought sacred, or return one day to find the home we dreamt of burning. But when the rain slows to a slant and the pavement turns cold, that place where I keep you and you and all of you—that place opens, like a fist no longer strong enough to stay closed. And the ache returns. Thank God. The sweet and sudden ache that lets me know I am alive. The rain keeps misting my face. What majesty of cells assembles around this luminous presence that moves around as me? How is it I'm still here? Each thing touched, each breath, each glint of light, each pain in my gut is cause for praise. I pray to keep falling in love with everyone I meet, with every child's eye, with every fallen being getting up. Like a worm cut in two, the heart only grows another heart. When the cut in my mind heals, I grow another mind. Birds migrate and caribou circle the cold top of the world. Perhaps we migrate between love and suffering, making our wounded-joyous cries: alone, then together, alone, then together. Oh praise the soul's migration. I fall. I get up. I run from you. I look for you. I am again in love with the world.

THREADING INNER
AND OUTER

The Practice of Journaling

Friend, I say,
since we are at death's
door, come in,
let us peer at Eternity
through the cracks
in each other's hearts.

R. S. THOMAS

I've always been a scribbler, and I've kept a journal of one kind or another for fifty years. I began journaling as a way to map and make sense of the many voices I felt moving through me. Most of this book comes from the river of perception spilling from one journal into the next, awash with a lifetime of feelings and questions. That river spans dozens of handwritten notebooks—small, large, pocketsize, hardcover, softcover.

As heartful, wakeful beings, we're conduits for the forces of life, which stream through us constantly. Keeping a journal became a way for me to relate to the life filling up my mind and heart. And like so much of life, once let out, secrets began to be knowable, pains began to lessen, and confusions began to clear. Over the years, the practice of journaling has served as a way to thread the inner life with the outer life, placing my soul more firmly in the world.

As a lifelong teacher, I've always used a journal as a tool to connect the inner lives of students with each other and the world. I would often stop in the middle of a conversation in class and say, "Journal Question!" Then I'd offer an invitation to explore some unanswerable depth, to see where it lived in their particular lives. Twice a semester, I'd meet individually with students to discuss their journals, the way archaeologists gather to examine what they've unearthed. I always respected my students' privacy. They were free to clip any passages they felt too personal to share, and I wouldn't read them. Yet I was always amazed at how eager they were to share it all. The life of the journal opened the class beyond a class. Through the journal, we became a small tribe of pilgrims.

When entered thoroughly, a journal can be an instrument for honest seeking and humble acceptance, the twin aerobics of the heart. And so I wholeheartedly encourage you to begin your own journal as a way to navigate the stream of your life.

IN RETURN TO PROMISE

(An Essay on Journaling)

THE ART OF CORRESPONDENCE

From the moment we open our eyes, after months in the unified world of the womb, we begin to correspond: to compare and contrast, to hold things up to each other, to see how things fit, to see how we fit. It may be as instinctual as thirst, or the need for warmth, or the need to cry. Our want to see how things go together is the way the human mind breathes. And at the end of all inquiry, like any combination of love and knowledge, we return to the feeling we were born with—Unity. Journaling is a canvas for our thoughts and feelings, a canvas for how things fit, for how we fit, for how we refind Unity. Journaling is how we stay in conversation with the Universe. Journaling is how we sketch truth with our heart.

In deep and lasting ways, journaling is how we practice the art of correspondence. The word *correspondence* consists of three root words: *cor*, meaning "together;" *re*, meaning "in return;" and *spondere*, meaning "to promise." So correspondence means: *together, in return to promise.* Where a diary is a place to track the circumstances of our life, a journal is a place to unfold the events that lift and drop us through our days, a place to ask all the questions that have no answer, a place to gather meaning from all we go through.

THE INHERENT SEQUENCE OF LEARNING

The threshold of all learning is question and response. And the gift of inquiry is that it draws an inner response from us. This is how we return to promise, how we turn into our possibility. By inquiring and inwardly responding, we become authentic. Real thinking is thought out loud, as real song is sung. And so real thinking involves question and response, which is at the heart of dialogue. When honest, we enter and engage true questions and stop seeking answers.

While the surface world requires certain answers—At what temperature does water freeze? Will diesel or unleaded gas fill up your car? And which foods are edible and which are poisonous?—the things that give us meaning—love, truth, paradox, and peace—are unanswerable. They reveal themselves when we are in relationship to them, not when we try to answer or solve them. A journal is a private, sacred place where we work out these relationships.

At the base of all learning is wonder. The chief task of our age, as teachers, seekers, and students, is to re-establish and reaffirm the inherent sequence of learning: to open wonder with a question, and then to respond; to see how things go together, and then to unify. As far back as Socrates, who led young Plato through the hills of Athens by trailing his questions like a path of honey, the use of question has been and remains the most untapped and most powerful learning tool there is. And any practice, instrument, experience, or technique that fosters the inherent sequence of learning is a significant aid in the art of living.

One such instrument is the journal. Its use is extremely versatile. It can serve as a fulcrum, mirror, lamp, or surveying tool. A journal tends to have a larger lens than a diary. A journal is more concerned with breaking trail and incorporating the unknown. A journal is a personal workspace of inwardness, a soul's log, a daybook of origins.

These descriptions all share one common assumption: there is something worth inquiring into, and something worth responding to. It's a fundamental belief on which all learning is based. There is something worthwhile and unique happening in each moment.

Frequently, we react to life before inquiring into life. The importance of a journal is that it actualizes who we are by exploring our relationship to everything we encounter. Once committed to the practice of reflection as a conduit between our soul and the Universe, a journal can animate our concerns and curiosities, providing a way to weave a tapestry of all the different strands of life.

We're always on a journey, and so there is always a space waiting to be entered. And the smallest effort will help us begin, even if we mutter to ourselves in the last moments of each day, even if we daydream in the dark before we drift to sleep. Whether we acknowledge it or not, the journey of learning, like the movement of air and light, never stops. We wake and look. We step and wonder. We question, then respond. We correspond, feel, and become real. What sketching is to a painter, journaling is to an awakened soul.

What, then, is the nature of this tool, the journal? It is daily, and therefore a way to exercise our attention. It is personal, and therefore a significant tie to the rest of life. It is a travel log of a soul's movement through the world. It is a book of original entry and therefore it reveals the truth that waits in anything—geography, the history of flowers, or the dynamics of your family. A journal is always concerned with origins, with where things begin and how things join.

Imagine a lifetime class of gifted students from all eras, and you have them read "The Fascination of What's Difficult" by William Butler Yeats. Then you ask them to identify and explore, in their journals, a process that fascinates them. In time, we would have a constellation of the remarkable journals written throughout history: Leonardo's notebooks, in which he conjectured accurately on the shape of the human fetus, centuries before the x-ray; Walt Whitman's *Specimen Days*, through which he recorded his life as a volunteer medic during the Civil War; Aldous Huxley's *The Doors of Perception*, in which he logged his experiments with mescaline; Anaïs Nin's diaries, in which the inner workings of love flare back to Sappho; Freud's case studies, through which he launched the world into modern psychology; Goethe's *Theory of Colors*, where he kept a daybook of his experiments with how light and dark affect our perceptions; John Reed's *Ten Days That Shook the World*, in which he served as an eye witness to the Russian Revolution; Thoreau's *Walden*, in which solitude wrestled its integrity from the modern world; James Baldwin's book-length essays, which are a fierce and tender journal of the mind; and of course, *The Diary of Anne Frank*, that somber knell that cracked the human bell.

There are more. And whether the ground of inquiry was science, the art of love, psychology, painting, alternate states of consciousness, history, or politics, the journal served them all. Adaptable. Durable. For just as exercise strengthens our muscles, our practice of question and reflection can enliven us, keeping us open, acute, perceptive, and thorough. By being faithful to the art of inner dialogue—searching for meaning in events, issues, ideas, and feelings—we can inhabit the one life we're given by engaging the world.

THE MANNER AND REACH OF THE JOURNAL

A journal seems to work best when established as a regular practice, in a daily way if possible. I would encourage you to regard it as an intimate place where you can enter time and bear witness to the miracle of life with all its wonders and hardships, where you can be honest about how life is whipping you around.

A journal is a place where you get to tell the truth as only you see it, even when you're wrong. I always enter my journal, as if no one will ever see it. I never consider a reader while diving so rawly into the questions of life. Only after retrieving whatever strands of meaning I can find, do I turn to sharing what I've found. Even then, I share with no intent other than to compare notes with the inwardness of others. What's most important is that your investigations remain honest, and so they must be done without any fear of invasion. Above all, it is your journal.

I also encourage you to make the space of your journal personal. So it matters what your journal looks like and feels like. It matters what you write with. Can your journal be carried around easily? Is it something you want to return to? It should be chosen the way you might choose a tennis racket, for its grip. I find that blank, hardbound artist sketchbooks are particularly welcoming. And your journal doesn't need to be well organized and logical. It doesn't need to be coherent or neatly gathered. Let your journal unfold organically in a way that mirrors the questions moving through your heart and mind. Your journal might look like Leonardo's, full of sketches and scribbling, full of tangents, hurriedly done in the heat of a moment's perception.

Generally, a journal is most effectively entered in three ongoing ways. It can be entered regularly by responding to the impact of your experiences. A second way to enter your journal is to respond to the things you read. I often enter my journal as if I'm in conversation with the voices I'm reading. When I'm moved by a poem by Rumi or a short story by Chekhov, I respond as if they've spoken to me and we're sitting somewhere quiet, having coffee.

A third way to enter your journal is by inquiring into a journal question. I'm always on the lookout for questions that stir me, that stir others, and so keep a list of questions, the kind that have no answers. Then I look them over and choose one to enter. I also encourage you not to press yourself to "finish" a journal question in one sitting. Rather, carry the question with you into life and be in conversation with the question more than once, so the question can weave you and life together.

Ultimately, true questions are carried like lanterns that we swing in the dark to help us find our way.

The Animated Life of Oneness

It can be expected initially that the space of a true journal will frighten us at times because it will open us to the depth of life. In a world where we've grown accustomed to separating what matters from what needs to be done, your journal might seem at first disorienting, because like a huge funnel it will draw things together in a whirl of integration.

This brings us back to our innate yearning for Unity, for the animated Life of Oneness, for what we have in common. And so, we return to the art of correspondence, to the effort to hold things up to each other, to see how things go together, to see how we fit. And be ready to be opened as you enter the depths. For this dive might change the way you view your life, the way you view all of life. You may have to allow other views in that you once thought didn't belong.

Sweating at the Dancer's Barre

We can't make anyone learn but ourselves. And so, I encourage you to work your journal like the barre and mirror a dancer works at, sweating and watching how the dance of who we are forms. By living closely to the heart of our experience, as we feel it in ourselves and in the world, we can enlarge our capacity. By living honestly, we can brush up against great moments of Oneness. And when we can accept how little we know, we can become authentic seekers. As Leonardo said, "The most important consideration in painting is that the movements of each figure express its inner state." Likewise, when we scribble and voice our deepest questions, feelings, and thoughts in our journals, we express our inner state and paint our very souls.

QUESTIONS TO WORK WITH

These journal questions have been gathered over the years from my own exploration of journaling and from my work as a teacher. They are starting points, dive spots if you will. Feel free to change them, combine them, undress them, and to voice questions of your own that these might stir, questions that might feel more relevant to what you're going through. These questions are invitations to better know yourself and to better relate to the currents of life. Each is a chance to personalize all that we have to face.

JOURNALING GUIDELINES

- I invite you to set aside time when you can enter what each question opens. This doesn't mean you can't begin with a five-or ten-minute window in your day. Whatever time you have, I encourage you to approach each question as a lookout you can return to, as you would the shore of a lake or a meadow on the edge of a mountain.

- When journaling, try not to select what to write about, but to open your heart and mind. Meditate on the question in silence for a minute or two and see what wants your heart's attention.

- Do not censor your writing. This is for you. It's more important that you be honest with yourself than hold back because someone else might see it.

- Allow form to follow content. Don't worry about organization or making sense, or even if you write in full sentences. Let your heart and deeper mind be your guide.

- Discover and enter what your thoughts and feelings point to, rather than summarizing what you already know.

- Journaling is a form of inquiry that leads to others: meditating, storytelling, being in conversation with others, and creating rituals. Let what surfaces in your journal lead you to embody its lessons in the weave of your life.

- Afterward, if it feels right, you can bring what you've uncovered into conversation with a loved one or trusted friend. If you're not comfortable sharing in this way, you can email a friend. It's also fine to experience these reflective moments in solitude.

- Remember, journal questions are experiments in authenticity. There is no right or wrong way to do this, no "normal" amount of time it takes, and no one way to enter.

- Trust whatever comes.

100 JOURNAL QUESTIONS

(Wherever possible, give personal examples.)

1. Which would you rather be, a mirror or a window, and why?

2. Describe which is more important and which is more difficult for you: explaining or understanding.

3. Explore whether you believe our choices matter or if everything is predetermined. Or do you feel that life is a mix of both?

4. Describe a friend you initially misjudged who later turned out to be steadfast and true.

5. What do we owe our ancestors? Can you personalize this question by speaking to a particular ancestor in your own lineage?

6. How responsible are we for others?

7. Can we do harm without being aware of the harm we cause? If so, what is the relationship between cruelty and awareness?

8. What kind of care is necessary to create love, maintain love, and protect love?

9. What is the difference, as you experience it, between your love of others and your love of work?

10. Describe the combination of care, freedom, knowledge, and need that makes up the kind of love you value? How is this different from the love you feel able to give?

11. In your experience, what is the difference between commitment and obligation? Explore a personal example of each.

12. Describe your commitment to the ones you love. Under what conditions would you stop loving?

13. Describe a situation where you had power over a loved one or were under the power of a loved one. What did each feel like? In your experience, how does power affect love?

14. Is there more power in touching or being touched? Is there more love in touching or being touched? Explain. Would you rather touch or be touched? Why? Would you rather be powerful or loved? Why?

15. Do you want power? What kind and why? What do you think power will do for you?

16. Define the most courageous decision you've made in your life to this point. What choices were available to you, and what makes what you did courageous?

17. Describe a situation in which you gave of yourself deeply without giving yourself away?

18. Describe a time when you acted without sympathy or compassion. What made you behave this way?

19. Describe a time when you were bewildered by life. What did you learn from this place of unknowing?

20. In your opinion, discuss if there is a perfect lover out there waiting for you or several compatible souls?

21. Where do you spend most of your time: in the past, present, or future? What leads you there?

22. Given your experience, would you rather understand flight or fly? Why?

23. Describe one inner quality you value that you were born with, that no one gave you.

24. Describe which is more reliable for you, your mind or your heart.

25. Name one aspect of life you'd like to experience more deeply.

26. Describe your relationship with someone who has a different view of God and the Universe than you.

27. Describe your relationship to a truth you believe in that has kept changing and evolving.

28. Describe an understanding of life that you stand on firmly, one that endures the storms that come your way.

29. If you could chose anyone not living from any time, who would you want to talk to, and what would you ask them?

30. Describe your personality as an aspect of nature.

31. What is your most serious goal in life right now, and what is your most playful goal? How do they inform each other?

32. Describe which quest you have chosen: perfection or fullness? Is this a choice you've made or one you've inherited?

33. Do you try to control the life around you or to immerse yourself in the life around you? What are the advantages and liabilities of both?

34. In what situations do you take more than you give? In what situations do you give more than you take? What are the rewards and costs of each?

35. How necessary is it to share something for it to have meaning?

36. Are you naturally introverted or extroverted? Are you comfortable with the way you meet the world?

37. Describe an instance when you had meaningful contact with an older person. How did this connection come about?

38. Describe your earliest memory in as much detail as possible.

39. What parts of you come from your mother and father?

40. Describe one specific trait you admire in your parents that you don't have.

41. Describe one specific trait you dislike in your parents that you do have.

42. When is it courageous to walk away and when is it cowardice?

43. Are you a joiner or a loner? Which would you like to be? If a joiner, where do you find your solitude? If a loner, where do you find your sense of belonging?

44. Describe someone you admire and the quality of their presence.

45. Do you believe everything in the Universe is connected, or do you feel the Universe is a collection of random parts? Explore your thinking around this and how your belief shapes how you move in the world.

46. Describe a time when you were too muddled in yourself.

47. Describe a time when you were too concerned about what others thought.

48. What do you aspire to? Explain whether this aspiration is based on internal or external goals.

49. Describe a situation where a lie was lived out though everyone really knew the truth.

50. In your opinion, who experiences and understands more of the world, the rich or the poor? In your opinion, why?

51. Describe a situation where you felt honor bound to some quest or understanding that no one else understood.

52. Which do you value more, the courage of your convictions or the courage of your tolerance? Which are you currently stronger at?

53. Describe a situation you got yourself into that was tough getting out of. What did you learn from entering this situation and from moving through it?

54. What does integrity mean to you? How do you practice it? Describe the most integral person you know.

55. Which has a greater impact on your identity, your memories or your expectations? Are you comfortable with this impact? How might you put some of your memories or expectations down?

56. Describe someone you like who is not like you, and why you like them.

57. How do you compare yourself to others? How do you understand your uniqueness?

58. How do you understand what you have in common with others? In your experience, what is at the heart of all people?

59. Describe an outlook or behavior that had a grip on you, which you have since left behind. Why did you let go of it, and how does it look from your current position?

60. Tell the story of a time when you felt ignored or rejected and what this did to your self-esteem. Describe your journey back to your self-worth. What led you away from yourself? What led you back?

61. Describe one thing you want that society wants for you.

62. Describe one thing you want that society doesn't want for you.

63. Do you make friends by approaching or being approached? How did you meet your best friend? Who reached out first?

64. In your experience, how is friendship actually built? In your opinion, what's the most important aspect of friendship?

65. Examine what you do for your career, or what you want to do for a career. What relation does it have to what you seek as a person? How does this career aid or hinder the awakening of your soul?

66. Do you want to know when you will die? Why?

67. Describe the largest Unity you believe in.

68. Throughout history, different precepts have been put forth as to how we can become complete. Classicism suggests that we can do so by looking outward and imitating the essential qualities of nature. Romanticism suggests that we can become whole through inwardness, by feeling and inhabiting our "inscape," as Gerard Manley Hopkins calls it. "Feeling is all," as the German poet Goethe says. By what process do you believe we can complete ourselves? Does it require interacting with the world or removing ourselves from the world? Please discuss.

69. Do we have any obligation to be a part of the world around us, be it human, natural, or universal? Why or why not?

70. What is lost and gained by losing innocence and ignorance? Give an example of something you lost and something you gained in your own coming of age.

71. Where do you find beauty, and where have you been taught to look for it? Explain the difference.

72. Read "The Fascination of What's Difficult" by William Butler Yeats. Then identify and explore a process in life that fascinates you.

73. How important is solitude to you?

74. Do you have an unseen side of your personality? Describe it and its last appearance in your life. How do you interact with this aspect of who you are?

75. A person pushes a stone all day without moving it at all. Is anything accomplished?

76. Is self-protection necessary? Why? Is the best self-protection being who you are or hiding who you are? Explain.

77. Given total freedom, what would you immerse yourself in, why, and toward what end?

78. In your own terms, define truth and describe the nature of its appearance.

79. Why do we seek the truth? Why do we tell the truth?

80. Describe the self you want to be. Describe the self you are. Explore the difference. What are you doing to move from one to the other?

81. Under what circumstances would you participate in a war? Why? Under what circumstances would you protest a war? Why?

82. What is the cost of going along: in love, in thought, in war? What is the cost of resistance: in love, in thought, in war?

83. Are the attitudes of war—such as seeking out the adversary, deceiving them, conquering them, taking prisoners, taking spoils, and imposing our values on the loser—at work in how we dream, love, pursue our careers, and sustain our families? Describe how. If not, what *is* at work in how we dream and live?

84. Does mature love between two people require giving up parts of who you are or maintaining the separation of two separate selves? Or some combination of both? Explore.

85. Explore what waits unlived in your heart and what you feel called to bring alive in the world.

86. Tell the story of a time when someone being hurtful triggered you to diminish yourself. Discuss how you could meet such a moment differently.

87. Identify a mood of frustration or sadness that you are currently struggling with. Without denying or minimizing your frustration or sadness, let your mind and heart open beyond your struggle and describe, if you can, some aspect of life around you that is not frustrating or sad. What does it feel like to allow both to take up space in you at the same time?

88. Describe a time when you gave up the language of your heart in order to be polite or to go along. How did this impact you? Then describe a time when you spoke from your heart regardless of the tensions going on around you. How did this impact you?

89. Tell the story of someone you admire who has been worn to their goodness.

90. Give an example of a phrase that has become part of your spiritual vocabulary. Tell the story behind this phrase. How does speaking or hearing this phrase affect you?

91. Describe a moment in which you fell into wild fields of silence. Where did it take you? How did you return? What do you take from the silence into your days?

92. Describe a moment of clarity in which you felt a greater sense of life than usual.

93. Identify someone you are close to who you play out unresolved issues with, and describe one such issue in detail. At a later time, if possible, present this issue to that person, owning your behavior and honoring their position in your life.

94. Describe a person who outgrew the name you had for them. Can you tell them so and ask what name they would like to be known by now?

95. Tell the story of a kindness you learned of long after it was given.

96. Talk about one thing dear to you that you've carried through the fire of life.

97. Describe how different parts of you have come together over time and how this new arrangement of your self has affected you.

98. Describe yourself as a painting half-finished by life. What colors are there? What is the painting of your life evoking? What world is your life a threshold to?

99. Describe a moment when you experienced complete compassion, when you were no longer separate from another person, animal, or part of nature. What led to this moment, and how has it opened your heart?

100. Tell the story of one important teacher who has shaped your life and how.

GRATITUDES

In essence, this entire book is a gratitude. For gratitude helps us face life. It is the sturdy bowl fired in the kiln of our experience. Drinking from that very personal and Universal bowl makes everything possible. In my life, there have been many who've held that bowl to my lips when I was too tired or tangled to find my way. More than I can say, but let me name a few.

I'm grateful to my agent, Jennifer Rudolph Walsh, for her kind and passionate creativity, as well as to Eve Attermann, Raffaella De Angelis, and the rest of the WME team for their outstanding support. I'm grateful to the Sounds True family for their care and excellence: especially Tami Simon for her belief in what we have to give, and to my editors there, Haven Iverson and Vesela Simic, and my producer Steve Lessard for the deep way they listen. And to Brooke Warner for her thoroughness of care. And to my publicist, Eileen Duhne, for the way she loves whatever she meets. And to Oprah Winfrey for her strength of heart.

Gratitude to my dear friends who always fill my bowl. Especially George, Don, Paul, Skip, TC, David, Kurt, Pam, Patti, Karen, Paula, Ellen, Linda, Michelle, Rich, Carolyn, Henk, Sandra, Elesa, and Joel and Sally.

And to Paul Bowler for always being there. And to Robert Mason for always encouraging me to look into the well under everything. And to my dear wife, Susan, who taught me how to fill another's heart.

MN

NOTES

E pigraphs and poems without attribution are by the author.

v "for Ryōkan . . ." Ryōkan Taigu (1758–1831) was a quiet Buddhist monk who lived much of his life as a hermit. Ryōkan is remembered for his poetry and calligraphy and for his love of Dogen (1200–1253), the Kyōtō-born teacher who founded the Sōtō school of Zen in Japan. Ryōkan was born in the village of Izumozaki in Echigo Province. He renounced the world at an early age to train at the nearby Sōtō Zen temple Kōshō-ji, refusing to meet with or accept charity from his family. He was originally ordained as Ryōkan Taigu. Ryō means "good," kan means "broad," and Taigu means "great fool." Ryōkan, the tender-hearted poet-monk, was known as a "broad-hearted generous fool." See Ryōkan's heartfelt poem "Reading the Record of Eihei Dogen" in *The Roaring Stream: A New Zen Reader*, edited by Nelson Foster and Jack Shoemaker (Hopewell, NJ: Ecco Press, 1996), 348.

"Neruda and the coal miner . . ." In his autobiography, *Memoirs*, the great Chilean poet Pablo Neruda (1904–1973) puts his fame and Nobel Prize in perspective when he tells of visiting a coal mine in his native Chile, where a miner came, soot-covered, from the bowels of the earth to grip his hand, saying, "I have known you a long time, my brother." The original Spanish title of Neruda's autobiography reads, *I Confess I Have Lived*. See *Memoirs* by Pablo Neruda, translated by Hardie St. Martin (New York: Farrar, Straus & Giroux, 1974).

"Whitman . . ." In December 1862, the legendary Walt Whitman (1819–1892) saw a list of wounded soldiers in the paper and was alarmed to find his brother there. During his journey to Washington to find his brother, Whitman saw many wounded and dead soldiers, which impacted him greatly. Once he found his brother alive, with minor injuries, Whitman stayed in Washington and began volunteering as a medic. Whitman's 1882 memoir, *Specimen Days*, recounts his experience of the Civil War. A now-anonymous review in *The Critic* (January 13, 1883) hails Whitman as "a Democratic Prometheus. . . . He is the painter who, unchastened by failures in the studio, rushes out into the fields and tries to paint a panorama of the whole horizon." See the Walt Whitman Archive (whitmanarchive.org/criticism/reviews/days/anc.00108.html) and the Electronic Text Center, from the University of Virginia Library, etext.virginia.edu/toc/modeng/public/WhiPro1.html.

"Rilke . . ." Rainer Maria Rilke (1875–1926) was a groundbreaking poet of the human interior. In addition to his lasting works, *Letters to a Young Poet* and *Duino Elegies*, his poem "The Panther" is haunting in how it explores the unconscious mood of captivity, which of course reverberates as a comment on our own unconscious captivity. From 1905 to 1906, Rilke worked as a secretary to the French sculptor Auguste Rodin, a remarkable meeting. It is believed that after being exposed to a small bronze tiger sculpted by Rodin, Rilke found his way to the Jardin des Plantes in Paris where he observed a live panther in captivity.

vii "We could all learn a lot from the flatfish . . ." from *Medusa's Children: A Journey from Newfoundland to Chiloé* (Regina, Saskatchewan: Coteau Books, 1993), 14. Lake Sagaris is a writer, community activist, and planner. She has lived in Santiago, Chile, for the past thirty years. She covered the movement for democracy against the Pinochet regime for the CBC, *The Globe and Mail, The Times* (London), the *Miami Herald*, and other media. Once the military regime ended (1990), she became active working on neighborhood issues and rebuilding democracy. As an elected leader of the Bellavista Neighbors Association, she was one of a group of twenty-five grassroots market and neighborhood associations that founded Living City (Ciudad Viva) in 2000. Since then, this award-winning organization has focused on transport for equality, recycling for local development, heritage for identity, and citizens' empowerment and democratic governance.

xvi The What and the How: "the sea of being that holds all feelings . . ." I explore this notion more deeply in the chapter "The Magic of Peace" in my book *The Endless Practice: Becoming Who You Were Born to Be* (New York: Atria Books, 2015).

9 epigraphs, Unraveling Our Fear: "I am troubled by my shapeless fears . . ." Vincent Van Gogh, quoted in "Sunbeams," *The Sun* 487 (July 2016): 48. And "I was born . . ." Rabia of Basra (717–801 CE) from *Love Poems from God: Twelve Sacred Voices from the East and West*, translated by Daniel Ladinsky (New York: Penguin, 2002), 7.

31 epigraph, The Gift of Deepening: "I can't explain or offer conclusions . . ." from a poem of mine, "The Festival of Life" in a book in progress called *Where All the Questions Live*.

35 Depth Seeks Us: This is the story of Eric Le Reste, the senior producer for Canadian Public Television's weekly show *Enquête*, a documentary-based program in investigative reporting. Eric is also deeply involved with the Brahma Kumaris, a worldwide spiritual path based on the mystical visions of its founder, Dada Lekhraj. I met and befriended Eric, a gentle and vibrant soul, at the Images and Voices of Hope Media Summit in 2011.

39 The Radiant Flow: "Let [yourself] look back on life . . ." Friedrich Nietzsche in *Untimely Meditations*, edited by Daniel Breazeale, translated by R. J. Hollingdale (England: Cambridge University Press, 1997).

39 "the Samurai who resigned . . ." Matsukura Ranran (1647–1693) was one of Bashō's oldest students and earliest disciples in Edo, famous for having resigned his position as a samurai to devote himself to poetry. The case of Matsukura and why he so dramatically changed his life serves as a koan for the archetypal choices we all face between thriving and surviving. For a more in-depth discussion of this, please see the chapter "The Troubles of Living" in my book *The Endless Practice: Becoming Who You Were Born to Be*. Matsukura died suddenly at the age of forty-seven. Lamenting his student's death, Bashō wrote this haiku (number 642):

        in autumn's wind,

        sadly broken,

        a mulberry staff.

47   The Privilege of Awe: "It is more important . . ." from
Petrarch's "On His Own Ignorance and That of Many
Others," quoted in *What Is Ancient Philosophy?* by Pierre Hadot,
translated by Michael Chase (Cambridge, MA: Harvard
University Press, 2002), xiii.

53   Love Is a Guess: Three titles found throughout this
book—"Love Is a Guess," "A Star after Rain," and "Time
Is a Rose"—are in tribute to lines from the poem "love is
a guess" by e. e. cummings, in *E. E. Cummings: Complete Poems
1904–1962*, edited by George James Firmage (New York:
Liveright, 1991), 1027.

71   epigraph, Navigating Trouble: "Let everything happen
to you . . ." Rainer Maria Rilke, quoted in "Sunbeams,"
The Sun 487 (July 2016): 48.

83   epigraph, Right-Sizing Our Pain: "For all these years . . ."
Rachel Reiland, quoted in "Sunbeams," *The Sun* 491
(November 2016): 48.

98   An Early Mirror: "the earliest remnants of mirrors we have . . ."
from "The Early Chinese Mirror" by Doris Dohrenwend. In
Artibus Asiae 27, no. 1/2 (1964): 79–98.

115   epigraph, The Radiance in All Things: "God does not
die . . ." from *Markings* by Dag Hammarskjöld, translated
by Leif Sjöberg and W. H. Auden (New York: Vintage
Books, 2006), 66.

123   The Oldest Song in the World: "These instruments date
back . . ." To listen to a recording of a reconstructed
prehistoric flute, visit openculture.com/2015/02/hear-the-
worlds-oldest-instrument-the-neanderthal-flute.html.

127   epigraphs, Burning Off What's Unnecessary: "Why must
the gate be narrow?" Wendell Berry, from "Sabbaths
1985, V" in *A Timbered Choir: The Sabbath Poems 1979–1997*
(Berkeley, CA: Counterpoint Press, 1998), 77. And "Joy is
the happiness . . ." Brother David Steindl-Rast, quoted in
"Sunbeams," *The Sun* 487 (July 2016): 48.

129 On the Edge of God's Shimmer: "Lives unlike mine . . ."
from *Red Suitcase* by Naomi Shihab Nye, (Brockport, NY:
BOA Editions, 1994), 80.

139 epigraph, Finding the Extraordinary in the Ordinary: "When
you wake up . . ." Dan Millman, quoted in "Sunbeams," *The
Sun* 389 (May 2008): 48.

149 epigraph, Always Building and Mending: "Into God's Temple
of Eternity . . ." Raymond Moriyama (born 1929) is a gifted
contemporary architect of Japanese descent. He has designed
several buildings at Brock University in Canada and is the
university's former chancellor.

161 epigraphs, The Strength of Our Attention: "I have a mind . . ."
Pablo Neruda, from the poem "Too Many Names," translated
by Alastair Reid, in *Pablo Neruda: Selected Poems*, edited by
Nathaniel Tarn (New York: Delta, 1970), 369. And "Our
heads are round . . ." This statement served as the title
of a retrospective exhibit, mounted at New York's Museum
of Modern Art (2016/2017), of the French leader of the
Dada movement, Francis Picabia (1879–1953) whose work
encompassed painting, poetry, publishing, performance, and film.

201 epigraph, Threading Inner and Outer: "Friend, I say . . ."
R. S. Thomas, from "The Survivors" in *Collected Poems
1945–1990* (London: Phoenix Press, 2002), 131.

PERMISSIONS

T hanks for permission to excerpt the following from other previously published works:

Quote from *Medusa's Children: A Journey*, Lake Sagaris (Regina, Saskatchewan, Canada: Coteau Books, 1993).

Passages in "Before We Die" first appeared as part of the article "The One Conversation," published online for *Super Soul Sunday* (OWN TV), January 19, 2012.

"The Only Task" first appeared as part of my essay in *The Dharma of Dogs: Our Best Friends as Spiritual Teachers*, edited by Tami Simon (Boulder, CO: Sounds True, 2017).

Excerpt from *A Timbered Choir: The Sabbath Poems 1979-1997*, Wendell Berry (New York: Counterpoint, 1999). Reprinted by permission of Counterpoint.

Excerpt from "First Hawaiian Bank" in *Red Suitcase*, Naomi Shihab Nye (New York: BOA Editions, Ltd., 1994). Reprinted with the permission of The Permissions Company, Inc., on behalf of BOA Editions, Ltd., www.boaeditions.org.

Excerpt from "Too Many Names," translated by Alastair Reid, in *Pablo Neruda: Selected Poems*, edited by Nathaniel Tarn (New York: Delta Books, 1970). Reprinted by permission of Delta Books.

Excerpt from *Collected Poems 1945-1990*, R.S. Thomas (London: Phoenix, 2002). Reprinted by permission of Orion Publishing Group.

About the Author

Mark Nepo moved and inspired readers and seekers all over the world with his #1 *New York Times* bestseller *The Book of Awakening*. Beloved as a poet, teacher, and storyteller, Mark has been called "one of the finest spiritual guides of our time," "a consummate storyteller," and "an eloquent spiritual teacher." His work is widely accessible and used by many, and his books have been translated into more than twenty languages. A bestselling author, he has published nineteen books and recorded fourteen audio projects. In 2015, he was given a Life Achievement Award by AgeNation. In 2016, he was named by *Watkins Mind Body Spirit* magazine as one of the 100 Most Spiritually Influential Living People, and was also chosen as one of OWN's SuperSoul 100, a group of inspired leaders who use their gifts and voices to elevate humanity. In 2017 Mark became a regular columnist for *Spirituality & Health* magazine.

Recent work includes *The Way Under the Way* (Sounds True, 2016), a Nautilus Book Award Winner; *The One Life We're Given* (Atria, 2016), cited by *Spirituality & Practice* as one of the Best Spiritual Books of 2016; *Inside the Miracle*, selected by *Spirituality & Health* magazine as one of the top-ten best books of 2015; *The Endless Practice*, cited by *Spirituality & Practice* as one of the Best Spiritual Books of 2014; *Reduced to Joy*, named by *Spirituality & Practice* as one of the Best Spiritual Books of 2013; as well as a six-CD box set of teaching conversations based on the poems in *Reduced to Joy*, and *Seven Thousand Ways to Listen*, which won the 2012 Books for a Better Life Award.

Mark was part of Oprah Winfrey's 2014 The Life You Want Tour and has appeared several times with Oprah on her *Super*

Soul Sunday program on OWN TV. He has also been interviewed by Robin Roberts on *Good Morning America*. *The Exquisite Risk* was listed as one of the Best Spiritual Books of 2005 by *Spirituality & Practice*, which called it "one of the best books we've ever read on what it takes to live an authentic life." Mark devotes his writing and teaching to the journey of inner transformation and the life of relationship. He continues to offer readings, lectures, and retreats. Please visit Mark at: marknepo.com, threeintentions.com, and info@wmeimgspeakers.com.